ROSS DOBSON

grillhouse

gastropub at home

MURDOCH BOOKS

— contents 03

» introduction

In recent times we have seen the grillhouse making what some may call a 'comeback'. This kind of gastropub-style food has often been unfairly represented as ironically-chic, very basic or even bordering on the comically retro. But I think this food actually deserves to be taken seriously. There is no doubt in my mind that there is an enduring sense of fun around this food — that may have been sidelined while it was replaced by some trendier, new kids on the block, but in its forced retirement, it somehow got street cred, was rehabilitated and clawed its way back.

And if we think of 'retro' food as the style of recipes from days gone by, this collection never really went anywhere. We've never stopped eating and enjoying classic, simple, hearty food. It may have been a while since it graced the covers of the foodie magazines but did people ever stop wanting to have a proper prawn cocktail, a perfectly roasted chicken or a juicy pepper steak?

Fads come and go and while this food is both fun and easy to make, it has also endured the test of time. It is simple, earnest and has endeared itself to us. It is about as up-front as food can be. I mean, could you get anything more classic than beef burgundy or steak and kidney pie or more honest than a prawn cutlet, potato gratin, cauliflower mornay or a piece of expertly grilled fish?

A rose by any other name would smell as sweet ... now who'd have thought I could reference Shakespeare when talking about grillhouse food? But that's just the thing, it's all about what it is and not what it's called. The grillhouse can mean many things to many people. Where I grew up there were several; The Wine Barrel, The Log Cabin, The Silver Grill. The latter was a restaurant where I worked as a nervous teen, made even more nervous by our uniform requirement of tight black pants, cumberbunds and flaming-red matador jackets. In this over-the-top garb, we had to attempt silver service for the unsuspecting customers while slicing smoked salmon and chateaubriand tableside. This aside, the chef would often give us samples from the menu and I couldn't get enough; pork medallions in creamy sauces, steaks cooked to perfection, lobster mornay and raspberry parfait. Though I have never worn a cumberbund since - I still really enjoy the food.

Fancy does not always have to mean tricky. With these recipes, any hard work involved is often able to be done well in advance like the pork terrine, potted prawns or salt cod fritters.

It's all about the prep. All you really need for a good steak is a hot grill and a few tips. Many of the accompaniments, butters and sauces can be made ahead of time and flavoured with garlic, curry, herbs or anchovies. Sauces are kept simple and classic; spiked with peppercorn, whisky cream, burnt butter and sage, or for a much simpler approach, you can occasionally mix this up with a few good-quality, ready-to-go sauces like Tabasco or a zesty mayonnaise. Marinades can do their trick overnight or within hours. Remember to be especially patient when grilling fish. Let the skin cook until crisp and golden on the grill before you even think of turning it over, and a sprinkling of sea salt and some freshly squeezed lemon is all you need to finish the dish off. There is no denying, however, that some recipes will require more thought and patience. Making a Bombe Alaska is not as simple as boiling an egg ... although, it is a far more fun and rewarding experience.

This is not an attempt at redefining food but rather a celebration of the classics. This collection of recipes includes dishes that are simple but rich, casual and fun with results that are very often posh but never snobby.

The grillhouse is not just retro or making a comeback — I don't think it really went anywhere in the first place.

It seems that the more the food costs, the less you need to fuss with it – take caviar and oysters as prime examples. This goes for all other good seafood and cuts of meat that require cooking. While cheap cuts of meat do need some slow cooking magic all we need do to a fillet steak or lobster is cook it quickly and serve it simply. Have the pan ready. Have the sides ready and you're almost there.

starters 13

The dessert is in the fridge. The main is ready for attention with some last minute prep – quick grilling, stirring, basting or braising. Getting the veggies ready. But let's not get ahead of ourselves. Enter the starter. The entrée to the meal. And really, who wants it to be such a fuss? Sure, you want it to look like you made an effort but let's make sure most of the work can be done in advance. Roll and crumb the crab cakes or cheese croquettes. Refrigerate the day before. Cooking them is all you now need do. Slice the beef for the carpaccio and make the dressing in advance. Put the chicken liver pâté in little pots and chill overnight. The flavour will only get better. Starters ... they're pretty much a done deal!

4–6 SERVINGS

1 tablespoon olive oil
2 rashers bacon, rind removed, cut into matchsticks
2 tablespoons finely diced red onion
2 tablespoons balsamic vinegar
1 tablespoon Worcestershire sauce
400 g (14 oz) rock salt
24 oysters, shucked
lemon wedges, to serve

» oysters kilpatrick

Heat the oil in a small non-stick frying pan over high heat. Add the bacon and stir-fry for 4–5 minutes until golden and crisp. Add the onion and cook for 2–3 minutes or until the onion has softened. Stir in the vinegar and cook for a few seconds or until nearly evaporated. Remove from the heat, then transfer it to a bowl and stir in the Worcestershire.

Preheat a grill (broiler) to high. Spread the rock salt over a baking tray, then place the oysters on top. Divide the bacon mixture among the shells. Cook under the grill for a short while — this depends on how far your oysters are from the heat, but you want the bacon to just start to sizzle. Serve with lemon wedges and a grind of black pepper.

150 g (5½ oz) unsalted butter, softened,
  plus 15 g (½ oz) extra
500 g (1 lb 2 oz) very small cooked prawns
  (shrimps), peeled, deveined and roughly
  chopped if slightly larger
1 tablespoon lemon juice
pinch each freshly grated nutmeg, white pepper
  and sea salt
buttered toast fingers, to serve

potted prawns «

Preheat the oven to 180°C (350°F/Gas 4).

Lightly butter four 170 ml (5½ fl oz) capacity ovenproof ramekins or serving bowls and place on an oven tray. Combine the prawns, lemon juice, nutmeg, pepper and salt in a bowl. Spoon the prawn mixture into the dishes, then firmly press down on the prawns with the back of a spoon. Put about 2 teaspoons of butter on each and bake for 10 minutes or until melted and heated through.

Meanwhile, place the remaining butter in a small saucepan and cook over low heat until melted, skimming off any white sediment that rises to the top. Pour the hot butter over the prawns, cool, then refrigerate for 2-3 hours or overnight. Serve directly from the dishes with buttered toast fingers.

4 SERVINGS

500 g (1 lb 2 oz) crabmeat
2 French shallots, finely chopped
2 tablespoons finely chopped coriander (cilantro)
½ teaspoon good-quality madras curry powder
2 tablespoons stale breadcrumbs
60 g (2¼ oz/¼ cup) good-quality mayonnaise
1 egg, lightly beaten
75 g (2½ oz/½ cup) plain (all-purpose) flour
250 ml (9 fl oz/1 cup) canola oil
coriander (cilantro) sprigs and lime wedges, to serve

» crab cakes

Pick over the crabmeat, removing any fragments of shell, then flake. Combine in a bowl with the shallot, coriander, curry powder, breadcrumbs and mayonnaise. Add the egg, season to taste and combine well. Cover and refrigerate for 3–6 hours. This mixture can be prepared up to one day ahead.

Using lightly floured hands, divide the mixture into 8 portions and shape into 5–6 cm (2–2½ in) round cakes.

Place the flour on a plate and season with salt and white pepper. Roll the cakes in the flour to coat all over.

Heat the oil in a non-stick frying pan over medium-high heat. When the surface of the oil is shimmering, add half the crab cakes and cook for 2–3 minutes on each side or until golden. Drain on paper towel, then repeat with the remaining cakes. Serve with coriander sprigs scattered over and lime wedges on the side.

40 g (1½ oz) butter
150 g (5½ oz/1 cup) plain (all-purpose) flour,
   plus 2 tablespoons extra
125 ml (4 fl oz/½ cup) milk
50 g (1¾ oz) cheddar cheese, grated
50 g (1¾ oz) mozzarella cheese, grated
½ teaspoon mustard powder
2 eggs

100 g (3½ oz/1 cup) stale coarse breadcrumbs
250 ml (9 fl oz/1 cup) canola oil
piccalilli or pickles, to serve

cheese croquettes »

Heat the butter in a small saucepan over high heat until sizzling. Stir in the 2 tablespoons extra flour and cook for 1 minute to make a thick paste. Remove from the heat and stir in the milk. Return to the heat and stir over medium heat for 1 minute or until thick and smooth. Add both cheeses, the mustard powder and ½ teaspoon of salt and stir until melted and smooth. Transfer to a bowl, cover closely with plastic wrap and refrigerate until cold.

Using lightly floured hands, divide the mixture into 8 portions. Form into small log-shaped croquettes, then place on a baking paper-lined tray. Place the remaining flour on a plate.

Place the eggs in a shallow bowl with 1 tablespoon of water and lightly beat. Place the breadcrumbs on another plate. Roll the croquettes in the flour to coat, then dip in the egg, allowing the excess to drain off, then roll in the crumbs to coat evenly. Place on a baking paper-lined tray, cover and refrigerate for 3 hours.

Heat the oil in a heavy-based frying pan over medium heat. Cook the croquettes, in 2 batches for 3-4 minutes, turning often, so they become an even golden colour all over. Serve with pickles or piccalilli for dipping.

4 SERVINGS

300 g (10½ oz) piece good-quality beef fillet, sinew removed
20 g (¾ oz) butter
60 ml (2 fl oz/¼ cup) olive oil
6 spring onions (scallions), finely chopped
½ teaspoon thyme leaves
pinch chilli flakes
2 tablespoons coarsely chopped toasted walnuts
1 tablespoon honey
125 ml (4 fl oz/½ cup) red wine vinegar
small handful rocket leaves

» beef carpaccio

Wrap the beef firmly in plastic wrap and place in the freezer for about 3 hours or until just firm.

Meanwhile, to make the walnut vinaigrette heat the butter and half the oil in a frying pan over medium heat. Add the spring onion and thyme and cook for 4–5 minutes or until soft and translucent. Add the chilli flakes and walnuts and cook for 1 minute, then add the honey and vinegar. Stir to combine well and simmer for 2–3 minutes or until reduced by about half. Remove from the heat and cool.

Using a sharp knife, slice the beef against the grain into very thin slices and arrange on 4 plates.

Scatter the rocket over the beef, spoon over the walnut vinaigrette, season with a little freshly ground black pepper and serve immediately.

6–8 SERVINGS

40 g (1½ oz) butter
1 onion, finely chopped
500 g (1 lb 2 oz) chicken livers, cleaned
pinch freshly grated nutmeg
½ teaspoon thyme leaves
40 ml (1¼ fl oz) brandy or Pernod
80 g (2¾ oz/⅓ cup) thick (double/heavy) cream
toasted baguette, cornichons and radicchio
    leaves, to serve

chicken liver pâté «

Heat the butter in a large heavy-based frying pan over medium heat. Add the onion and cook for 5 minutes or until soft. Add the livers, nutmeg, thyme and 1 teaspoon salt and cook, shaking the pan, for 2–3 minutes or until the livers are browned but not cooked through. Increase the heat to high, add the brandy and stir for 1 minute. Stir in the cream and remove from the heat. Set aside for 10–15 minutes.

Process the liver mixture until smooth — don't worry if there are still a few lumps left. Press the mixture through a fine sieve placed over a bowl. Spoon into a 500 ml (17 fl oz/2 cup) capacity bowl, cover closely with plastic wrap and refrigerate overnight.

Remove from the refrigerator 1 hour before serving. Serve with slices of toasted baguette, cornichons and radicchio leaves.

4 SERVINGS

½ teaspoon hot smoked paprika
¼ teaspoon cayenne pepper
½ teaspoon ground cumin
1 teaspoon sea salt flakes
1.5 litres (52 fl oz/6 cups) canola or vegetable oil
65 g (2½ oz/½ cup) potato flour
500 g (1 lb 2 oz) small raw school
   prawns (shrimp), unpeeled
lemon wedges, to serve

PAPRIKA MAYONNAISE
185 g (6½ fl oz/¾ cup) good-quality mayonnaise
1 teaspoon sweet smoked paprika
2 cloves garlic, crushed
2 teaspoons lemon juice

» spiced school prawns with paprika mayonnaise

For the paprika mayonnaise, combine all the ingredients in a bowl, cover and refrigerate until needed.

Place the paprika, cayenne, cumin and sea salt in a small frying pan over medium heat. Shake the pan over the heat for 2–3 minutes or until the spices are aromatic and nearly smoking but not burnt. Pour into a bowl and stand until cool.

Place the oil in a wok or wide saucepan over high heat. Test if the oil is ready by sprinkling a pinch of the potato flour into the oil. It should sizzle on contact.

Have a bundle of paper towels ready to drain the cooked prawns on. Put one third of the prawns in a colander or sieve and sprinkle over one-third of the potato flour. Shake the prawns around in the sieve so they are coated in the flour and the excess is shaken off. Carefully add to the oil and cook for 2 minutes or until pink and starting to turn golden. Use a slotted spoon or small sieve and remove to the paper towel to drain. Repeat with the remaining prawns and flour.

Put all the cooked prawns in a large metal bowl. Sprinkle over the spice mixture and toss to coat well. Serve immediately with the paprika mayonnaise, lemon wedges and finger bowls.

4 SERVINGS

150 g (5½ oz) jar oysters
40 g (1½ oz) butter
2 thick rashers bacon, thinly sliced
1 onion, finely chopped
1 clove garlic, crushed
1 bay leaf
½ teaspoon thyme leaves
1 tablespoon plain (all-purpose) flour
500 ml (17 fl oz/2 cups) seafood or fish stock

2 large all-purpose potatoes (such as desiree),
    peeled and diced
400 g (14 oz/2 cups) good-quality seafood
    marinara mix
125 ml (4 fl oz/½ cup) pouring (whipping) cream
handful roughly chopped flat-leaf (Italian)
    parsley leaves
crusty bread, to serve

» seafood chowder

Drain the oysters and reserve 60 ml (2 fl oz/¼ cup) of the liquid.

Melt the butter in a heavy-based saucepan over medium heat and cook the bacon for 5 minutes. Add the onion and cook for another 5 minutes or until the onion is soft and the bacon is crisp. Stir in the garlic, bay leaf and thyme and cook for 1 minute or until aromatic. Sprinkle over the flour and stir for 1 minute, or until everything is well coated in flour. Gradually add the reserved oyster liquid and the stock and whisk to combine for 2–3 minutes. Add the potatoes and bring to a simmer. Cook for 15–20 minutes or until the potatoes are tender.

Add the marinara mix and cook for 2–3 minutes or until the seafood is just cooked. Stir in the cream, oysters and parsley and cook for 1 minute or until the oysters are just warmed through. Season with salt and freshly ground black pepper to taste and serve with crusty bread.

4 SERVINGS

TARTARE SAUCE
3 egg yolks, at room temperature
1 tablespoon lemon juice
¼ teaspoon green Tabasco sauce
185 ml (6 fl oz/¾ cup) light olive oil
1 tablespoon salted capers, rinsed and
  finely chopped
1 tablespoon finely chopped dill pickle
1 tablespoon chopped flat-leaf (Italian) parsley

500 g (1 lb 2 oz) skinless, firm white fish fillets
150 g (5½ oz/1 cup) plain (all-purpose) flour
1 teaspoon baking powder
250–300ml (9–10½ fl oz) ice-cold beer
canola oil, for deep-frying
60 g (2¼ oz/½ cup) cornflour (cornstarch)
sea salt flakes and lemon wedges, to serve

blue eye fish cocktails « with tartare sauce

Cut the fish into bite- sized pieces.

Combine the flour, baking powder and ½ teaspoon salt in a bowl, then make a well in the centre. Whisk in 250 ml (9 fl oz/1 cup) beer until smooth. The batter should be the consistency of thick cream. Add a little more beer if necessary. Set aside for 15 minutes.

Meanwhile, for the tartare sauce, place the egg yolks, lemon juice, Tabasco and a pinch of salt in a small bowl. Place a wet dish cloth on a work bench and sit the bowl on top. This will allow you to use both your hands to whisk and add oil at the same time without the bowl moving too much. Start to whisk the egg yolk mixture and as you do add a thin stream of the oil. Keep whisking and adding the oil until all the oil has been added and the mixture is thick and emulsified. Stir in the capers, pickle and parsley and check the seasoning.

Pour enough oil into a wok or large saucepan to come halfway up the sides and place over medium-high heat. The oil is ready when the surface is shimmering or a small amount of batter sizzles upon contact.

Place the cornflour in a bowl. Working in small batches, add some of the fish pieces to the cornflour and toss to coat, then shake off the excess. Using a pair of tongs or chopsticks, dip the fish cocktails into the batter, allow the excess to drain, then carefully place into the oil. Cook, turning with tongs, for 2-3 minutes or until golden and crisp. Drain on the paper towel, then sprinkle with sea salt and serve with lemon wedges and tartare sauce.

4 SERVINGS

20 g (¾ oz) butter
2 cloves garlic, finely chopped
2 French shallots, finely chopped
1 celery stalk, finely diced
2–3 sprigs thyme
1 bay leaf
250 ml (9 fl oz/1 cup) fish stock
2 kg (4 lb 8 oz) black mussels, cleaned
125 ml (4 fl oz/½ cup) thick (double/heavy) cream
handful flat-leaf (Italian) parsley leaves, coarsely chopped
warm crusty bread, to serve

» mussels marihières

Melt the butter in a wide saucepan or deep frying pan over medium heat. Add the garlic, shallots and celery and cook for 2-3 minutes or until soft. Stir in the thyme and bay leaf and increase the heat to high. Add the stock and bring to the boil. Add the mussels, cover the pan and cook, shaking the pan often, for 2-3 minutes or until the mussels just start to open. Avoid cooking any longer or the mussels will shrivel up and toughen. Discard any that do not open. Stir in the cream and parsley, season to taste and serve with warm crusty bread.

2 large avocados
2 lemons, cut into wedges
20 cooked prawns (shrimp), peeled and deveined

DRESSING
2 egg yolks, at room temperature
pinch freshly ground white pepper
2 teaspoons lemon juice
125 ml (4 fl oz/½ cup) light olive oil
2 tablespoons thick (double/heavy) cream
1 teaspoon Worcestershire sauce
¼ teaspoon green Tabasco sauce

prawn & avocado cocktail »

For the dressing, place the egg yolks, white pepper and lemon juice in a small bowl. Place a wet dish cloth on a work bench and sit the bowl on top. This will allow you to use both hands to whisk and add oil at the same time without the bowl moving too much. Start to whisk the egg yolk mixture and, as you do, add a thin stream of the oil. Keep whisking and adding the oil until the mixture becomes thick and emulsified.

Stir in the cream and sauces, season to taste, then cover and refrigerate until needed.

Cut the avocados in half and remove the stone. Use a large metal spoon to scoop out the flesh in one piece and cut into large pieces. Squeeze a little lemon juice over the top. Divide the avocado among 4 small bowls, top with the prawns and spoon over the dressing.

4 SERVINGS

1.5 kg (3 lb 5 oz) roma (plum) tomatoes
6 cloves garlic, peeled
1 red onion, cut into thick wedges
1 long red chilli, roughly chopped
2 large sprigs rosemary
125 ml (4 fl oz/½ cup) light olive oil
2 anchovies, mashed with the back of a fork
250 ml (9 fl oz/1 cup) chicken or vegetable stock
110 g (3¾ oz/½ cup) mascarpone
extra virgin olive oil, for drizzling
toasted crusty bread, to serve

» roasted tomato soup

Preheat the oven to 220°C (425°F/Gas 7).

Cut the tomatoes in half and arrange, cut side up, on a baking paper-lined oven tray. Scatter with the garlic, onion, chilli and rosemary. Drizzle with half the oil and bake for 30 minutes or until the tomatoes have collapsed. Allow to cool for 15 minutes.

Discard the rosemary, then place the tomato mixture and the anchovies in a food processor and process until roughly chopped and chunky. Transfer to a saucepan. Add the stock and simmer over medium heat for 20 minutes or until slightly thickened. Ladle into bowls and serve with a dollop of mascarpone, a drizzle of extra virgin olive oil and crusty bread.

16 golf-ball-sized beetroots
2 tablespoons extra virgin olive oil
1 teaspoon red wine vinegar
½ teaspoon wholegrain mustard
80 g (2¾ oz) frisée
50 g (1¾ oz/½ cup) walnuts, lightly toasted
8 thin slices of baguette, cut on the diagonal
100 g (3½ oz) firm goat's cheese, sliced into
    8 pieces

goat's cheese toasts with « beetroot & walnut salad

Bring a saucepan of lightly salted water to the boil and cook the beetroot for 25–30 minutes or until tender when pierced with a fork. Drain well and, when cool enough to handle, slip off the skins and discard. Cut any larger beetroots in half and transfer to a bowl.

Combine the oil, vinegar and mustard in a small bowl. Pour half over the warm beetroot and stir to combine.

Preheat a grill (broiler) to medium.

Arrange the frisée and beetroot on a serving platter and sprinkle over the walnuts. Drizzle over the remaining dressing.

Toast one side of the baguette slices under the grill until golden. Put a slice of goat's cheese on the untoasted side and toast until melted. Arrange the toasts on the salad or serve on the side.

4–6 SERVINGS

1 kg (2 lb 4 oz) chicken wings
2 cloves garlic, crushed
60 ml (2 fl oz/¼ cup) extra virgin olive oil
2 tablespoons dijon mustard
45 g (1½ oz/¼ cup) soft brown sugar
2 tablespoons Worcestershire sauce
2 tablespoons balsamic vinegar
1 teaspoon cayenne pepper
1 teaspoon sweet paprika

» devilled chicken wings

Cut the tips off the wings and discard. Using a large knife, cut between the joints to give two pieces from each wing. Place the chicken and the remaining ingredients in a large non-metallic bowl or ziplock bag. Stir or shake the bag well to combine. Refrigerate for at least 6 hours, or preferably overnight, stirring often.

Preheat the oven to 180°C (350°F/Gas 4) and line one large or two smaller baking trays with baking paper.

Place the wings in a single layer on the tray/s, making sure they are not overcrowded or overlapping. Cook for 30 minutes, then turn over and cook for another 20 minutes or until golden and sticky.

500 g (1 lb 2 oz) boneless pork belly, skin on
500 g (1 lb 2 oz) minced (ground) pork
1 clove garlic, crushed
1 teaspoon thyme leaves
small handful finely chopped flat-leaf
    (Italian) parsley
2 teaspoons finely grated orange zest
60 ml (2 fl oz/¼ cup) brandy
½ teaspoon caster (superfine) sugar
1 egg, lightly beaten
8–10 rashers bacon
toasted bread and tamarind relish, to serve

simple pork terrine «

Use a sharp knife to remove the pork skin from the pork belly and then discard. Cut the pork belly into 1 cm (½ in) pieces. Place in a bowl with the minced pork, garlic, thyme, parsley, zest, brandy, sugar and 1 teaspoon sea salt and use clean hands to combine well. Cover and refrigerate for at least 12 hours, mixing with your hands every 6 hours or so.

Preheat the oven to 160°C (315°F/Gas 2-3).
Remove the pork mixture from the refrigerator and set aside for 30 minutes. Add the egg, then use your hands to combine really well. Stand for 15 minutes. Line a 20 x 7 x 8 cm (8 x 2¾ x 3¼ in) deep loaf (bar) tin with the bacon rashers, so they slightly overlap and overhang the sides. Place the pork mixture in the tin and fold the overhanging bacon over the top. Cover firmly with 2 layers of foil and place in a deep roasting pan. Add enough water to come as close to the top of the loaf tin as possible. Transfer the tin to the oven and cook for 1¾ hours. Remove from the oven and allow the terrine to cool in the water bath for 3 hours. Serve at room temperature or refrigerate. Remove from the refrigerator 30 minutes before serving, sliced with toasted bread, relish and pickles.

Not too much mucking around — that's what we want from a starter, whether we're making it or eating it. This means lots of fresh seafood: oysters grilled in the shell with some bacon; little potted prawns; scallops; fish cocktails and spiced school prawns. This food does not require much knife and fork action. This is food you use your hands to eat. Shared, dig-in-and-don't wait-food. Leave manners aside and eat that extra scallop or fish cocktail. Napkins a plenty. Next course please!

12 SCALLOPS

20 g (¾ oz) unsalted butter
1 tablespoon plain (all-purpose) flour
125 ml (4 fl oz/½ cup) milk
50 g (1¾ oz) grated gruyère cheese
12 scallops on the half shell
finely chopped flat-leaf (Italian) parsley, to serve

» scallop mornay

Heat the butter in a small saucepan over medium heat. When sizzling and melted, add the flour and stir for 1 minute. Remove from the heat and whisk in the milk. Stirring continuously, cook over low heat for 2-3 minutes or until the sauce is thick and resembles a custard. Add the cheese and stir until melted and smooth, season to taste, then remove from the heat.

Preheat a grill (broiler) to high heat and adjust the setting so the scallops will be at least 5 cm (2 in) from the heat.

Place the scallops in their shells in a single layer on an oven tray. Spoon a little sauce over each scallop, then grill for 2-3 minutes or until the sauce is bubbling and golden. Sprinkle over the parsley and serve immediately.

12 SCALLOPS

12 scallops on the half shell
250 g (9 oz) cauliflower florets
1 tablespoon thick (double/heavy) cream
2 rashers bacon, rind removed, cut into
  matchsticks
2 tablespoons olive oil

scallops with cauliflower « purée & bacon

Remove the scallops from the shell. Rinse the scallops and the shells, drying both well.

Bring a saucepan of salted water to the boil and cook the cauliflower for 8–10 minutes or until very tender. Drain well, then place in a food processor with the cream and process until smooth. Season to taste.

Preheat the grill (broiler) to high and adjust the setting so the scallops will be at least 5 cm (2 in) from the heat. Place the shells in a single layer on an oven tray.

Spoon a little cauliflower purée into each shell, then place a scallop on top of the purée and sprinkle with a little bacon. Drizzle each scallop with a little olive oil then grill for 2–3 minutes or until the bacon is crisp and the purée is starting to turn golden and bubbling. Sprinkle with a little freshly ground black pepper and serve immediately.

grilled

Grilled – it is as it says. So it wouldn't be a bad idea to invest in a barbecue or at least a heavy cast-iron grill plate or skillet to cook indoors. And you need it to be hot, really hot, to get that seared and charred bistro result. There are not too many tricks to grilling, yet the few rules that do exist are well worth remembering and adhering to.

When cooking with any red meat, take it out of the fridge for a short while prior to cooking, letting it come to room temperature. Many of the cuts of meat we grill – the sirloins, the lamb chops, the t-bones and fillet steaks do not require long cooking times and are often best a little pink in the centre.

4 SERVINGS

4 sirloin steaks, about 200 g (7 oz) each
1 tablespoon light olive oil
sea salt

BÉARNAISE
3 egg yolks
1 tablespoon tarragon vinegar
60 ml (2 fl oz/¼ cup) light olive oil
200 g (7 oz) butter

» sirloin steak with béarnaise

For the béarnaise, place the egg yolks and vinegar in a small food processor. With the motor running, gradually add the oil in a very slow, steady stream until all the oil has been added and the mixture is thick and emulsified. Place the butter in a small saucepan and cook over high heat until melted and sizzling. With the motor running again, pour the hot butter into the mayonnaise in a thin steady stream and process until thick and smooth. This can be made several hours in advance, then transferred to a warmed thermos where it will keep warm for 2 hours. Makes about 310 ml (10¾ fl oz/1¼ cups).

Brush the steaks with the oil and put on a plate. Season the tops with sea salt and freshly ground black pepper to taste. Stand at room temperature for 30 minutes.

Heat a chargrill or barbecue flat plate to high. When smoking hot, add the steaks, seasoned side down, and cook for 4 minutes. Season the other side to taste, then turn and cook for another 4 minutes for medium rare. This will vary according to the thickness of the steaks. Remove, cover loosely with foil and rest for 5 minutes.

Spoon over the béarnaise to serve.

4 SERVINGS

12 lamb chops
2 tablespoons olive oil
4 sprigs rosemary

ANCHOVY BUTTER
1 vine-ripened tomato
125 g (4½ oz) unsalted butter, softened
1 clove garlic, crushed
2 anchovies, finely chopped
1 tablespoon finely chopped flat-leaf (Italian) parsley

» lamb chops with anchovy butter

Place the lamb chops, olive oil, rosemary and salt and pepper to taste in a dish. Toss to combine well, then cover and set aside for 1 hour.

Meanwhile, for the anchovy butter, remove the stem from the tomato and cut out the core. Cut a small and shallow cross on the opposite end and place in a small heatproof bowl. Pour enough boiling water over the tomato to cover, then stand in the hot water for 1 minute or until the skin starts to peel. Remove the tomato, refresh in iced water and peel the skin. Cut in half and scoop and discard all the seeds, then cut the flesh into a small dice. Place the tomato, butter, garlic, anchovies and parsley in a bowl and stir to combine well.

Lay a sheet of plastic wrap on a work surface and spoon the anchovy butter down the centre. Roll the butter up in the plastic to make a log, twisting the ends to seal. Refrigerate until needed, up to a day in advance.

Preheat a chargrill to high. When smoking hot, cook the lamb chops for 3 minutes on each side. Transfer to a plate, cover loosely with foil and rest for 5 minutes. Slice the anchovy butter into thin coins and serve on the lamb.

4 rump steaks, about 200 g (7 oz) each
olive oil, for brushing
lime wedges, to serve

TABASCO BUTTER
125 g (4½ oz) unsalted butter, softened
   to room temperature
¼ teaspoon green Tabasco sauce
1 small clove garlic, crushed
1 tablespoon finely chopped flat-leaf
   (Italian) parsley
1 tablespoon finely chopped coriander (cilantro)

rump steak with «
tabasco butter

For the Tabasco butter, place all the ingredients and a pinch of sea salt in a bowl and combine well. Lay a sheet of plastic wrap on a work surface. Spoon the butter mixture down the centre to make a log about 10 cm (4 in) long. Firmly wrap the butter up in the plastic to make a log. Refrigerate until needed. This can be made up to 2 days in advance.

Lightly brush the steaks with oil and season well with sea salt and freshly ground black pepper.

Preheat a chargrill to high. When smoking hot, cook the steaks for 3 minutes on each side for medium rare. Transfer to a plate, cover loosely with foil and rest for a couple of minutes.

Slice the Tabasco butter into thin coins and serve on the warm steaks with lime wedges on the side.

130 g (4¾ oz) salt
35 g (1¼ oz) sugar
3 large pork loin fillets, about 400 g (14 oz) each
2 tablespoons light olive oil
1 tablespoon smoked sweet paprika
125 ml (4 fl oz/½ cup) maple syrup

pork loin with maple « paprika glaze

Place the salt, sugar and 2.5 litres (84 fl oz/ 10 cups) of water in a large stainless steel saucepan and stir over low heat until the salt and sugar have dissolved. Remove from the heat and cool completely. Add the pork fillets, cover and set aside for 3 hours.

Remove the pork, and pat dry with paper towel. Combine the olive oil and paprika in a small bowl and rub all over the pork.

Preheat a chargrill to medium. Lay two sheets of baking paper on the grill. This will prevent the glaze from burning. Cook the pork for 10-12 minutes, turning every 2 minutes until well browned all over. Reduce the heat to medium. Start brushing the pork lightly with the maple syrup, turning the pork each time the surface has been brushed. Cook and brush for another 2-3 minutes, adjusting the heat if the glaze starts to burn, until the pork is dark golden.

Transfer to a plate, cover loosely with foil and rest for 5 minutes before slicing.

4 SERVINGS

4 fillet steaks, about 180 g (6½ oz) each
50 g (1¾ oz) unsalted butter
1 tablespoon olive oil
1 clove garlic, finely chopped
1 tablespoon plain (all-purpose) flour
125 ml (4 fl oz/½ cup) white wine
125 ml (4 fl oz/½ cup) beef stock
2 tablespoons green peppercorns in brine, drained
60 g (2¼ oz) thick (double/heavy) cream

» steak with green peppercorn sauce

Pound the steaks lightly until they are an even 1 cm (½ in) thickness all over. Season both sides well with salt and pepper and set aside for 30 minutes.

Heat the butter and oil in a large heavy-based frying pan over high heat. When the butter is sizzling and almost smoking hot, but not burnt, add the steaks and cook for just 2 minutes on each side. Remove from the pan.

Add the garlic to the pan and cook for just a few seconds or until aromatic but not burnt.

Add the flour and stir to combine with the pan juices, scraping the bottom of the pan to remove any sediment. Add the wine and stir for 1 minute or until thickened, then add the stock and peppercorns and bring to the boil, stirring regularly. Reduce the heat to low and simmer for 2 minutes, then add the cream, season to taste and stir until well combined. Return the steaks and any resting juices to the pan for a minute, turn to coat in the sauce, then serve.

4 SERVINGS

125 ml (4 fl oz/½ cup) red wine
4 sprigs thyme
6 cloves garlic, peeled and crushed with the
   back of a knife
4 fillet steaks, about 150 g (5½ oz) each
2 small raw lobsters, halved
2 cloves garlic, finely chopped
85 g (3 oz) butter
2 teaspoons finely chopped flat-leaf
   (Italian) parsley
1 tablespoon olive oil

posh surf & turf «

Combine the red wine, thyme and garlic in a non-metallic bowl. Add the steaks, toss to coat, then cover and refrigerate for 3 hours. Remove from the refrigerator 1 hour before cooking.

Place the lobster halves on an oven tray. Place the garlic and 65 g (2¼ oz) butter in a small saucepan over medium heat. When the butter just starts to sizzle, remove the pan from the heat and stir through the parsley. Brush half the butter mixture over the lobster meat and set aside while cooking the steaks.

Preheat a grill (broiler) to high.

Heat the oil in a heavy-based frying pan over high heat. Add the steaks and cook for 1 minute on each side. Reduce the heat to medium and cook for another 2 minutes on each side for medium-rare. Add the remaining butter, letting it sizzle in the pan for 1 minute and spoon over the steaks. Transfer the steaks to a plate, cover loosely with foil and rest for 5 minutes.

Cook the lobsters under the grill for 5 minutes, basting every minute with the remaining butter mixture, until the flesh is opaque and cooked through. Serve side by side the steaks.

4 SERVINGS

4 thick t-bones steaks, about 400 g (14 oz) each
2 cloves garlic, peeled and halved
olive oil, for brushing
sea salt
70 g (2½ oz) butter
4 French shallots, thinly sliced
125 ml (4 fl oz/½ cup) white wine
125 ml (4 fl oz/½ cup) veal or beef stock
handful flat-leaf (Italian) parsley leaves, finely chopped
2 teaspoons lemon juice

» t-bone with bercy sauce

Rub both sides of the steaks, including the bones, with the garlic cloves. Lightly brush the steaks with oil, season with sea salt and freshly ground black pepper and set aside.

Melt 50 g (1¾ oz) butter in a small frying pan over high heat. Add the shallots and cook, stirring regularly for 4–5 minutes or until soft. Add the wine and let it sizzle and reduce by about half. Add the stock, parsley and lemon juice and cook for a couple of minutes, then stir through the remaining 20 g (¾ oz) butter and remove from the heat. Season to taste.

Heat a chargrill on high. When hot, cook the steaks for 4 minutes each side for rare.

Transfer the steaks to a plate, cover loosely with foil and rest for 5 minutes.

Reheat the sauce on low heat for 1 minute, then pour over the steaks and serve.

4 SERVINGS

4 flounder, about 600 g (1 lb 5 oz) each
2 tablespoons olive oil
sea salt
100 g (3½ oz) butter
24 small sage leaves
lemon wedges, to serve

whole flounder with «
burnt butter & sage sauce

Rinse the flounder and pat dry well with paper towel. Rub the top side of the flounder with the oil and season well with sea salt and freshly ground black pepper.

Preheat the oven to 180°C (350°F/Gas 4) and a barbecue flat plate to high.

Tear off a large sheet of baking paper and place on the flatplate. Place the fish on the baking paper, top side down, and cook for 5 minutes. Turn the fish over and cook for another 5 minutes, then place, top side up, on an oven tray and bake for 5 minutes. Remove from the oven and transfer to warm serving plates and cover loosely with foil.

Melt the butter in a frying pan over medium heat, swirling the pan around so it melts evenly. Add the sage leaves and cook until the sage leaves crispen and the butter starts to froth and become nutty and aromatic. Remove from the heat before the sediment in the bottom of the pan starts to burn. Spoon the hot butter over the fish and serve with lemon wedges on the side.

4 SERVINGS

4 veal cutlets, about 250 g (9 oz) each
2 cloves garlic, roughly chopped
2 anchovies, finely chopped
80 ml (2½ fl oz/⅓ cup) olive oil
1 tablespoon lemon juice
1 lemon, thinly sliced
12–15 sage leaves, sliced
1 tablespoon small salted capers, well rinsed and drained
60 ml (2 fl oz/¼ cup) white wine

» veal cutlets with sage, capers & lemon

Place the veal in a non-metallic dish with the garlic, anchovies, 2 tablespoons olive oil, lemon slices and the lemon juice. Toss the cutlets around so they are coated in the mixture and set aside for 1 hour.

Heat a large heavy-based frying pan over high heat. Lift the cutlets and lemon slices out of the marinade, wiping off excess marinade so it collects in the dish to be used later. Season the cutlets to taste, then cook for 4–5 minutes each side, until golden and the fat has crisped up. Transfer the cutlets to a plate, and cover loosely with foil. Cook the lemon slices for 1 minute on each side or until lightly caramelised.

Add the remining olive oil to the pan, then add the sage leaves, capers and cook for 2–3 minutes, turning the lemon slices once, until golden and soft. Add the wine and cook for another minute, letting it sizzle and reduce. Add the reserved marinade and cook, stirring to remove any sediment, for 2–3 minutes or until the sauce is slightly thickened. Pour over the cutlets to serve.

4 SERVINGS

4 fillet steaks, about 150–180 g (5½–6 oz) each
1 tablespoon black peppercorns
1 tablespoon white peppercorns
1 teaspoon sea salt flakes
1 tablespoon light olive oil
40 g (1½ oz) butter
1 tablespoon brandy

steak au poivre »

Remove the steaks from the refrigerator and set aside for about 30 minutes while preparing the pepper rub.

Place the peppercorns in a spice mill or mortar and pestle and crush to a coarse powder. Pour the peppercorns into a fine sieve, then shake off and discard all the fine powder. Tip the remnants from the sieve onto a plate. Press both sides of the steaks onto the crushed peppercorns to coat. Sprinkle the steaks on both sides with the salt, then place on a wire rack and set aside for 30 minutes.

Heat the oil in a large heavy-based frying pan over high heat. When smoking hot, add the steaks and cook for 2 minutes. Reduce the heat to medium and cook for another 3 minutes. Turn the steaks over, increase the heat to high and repeat, cooking the steaks for 2 minutes, then reducing the heat to medium and cooking for another 2 minutes for medium-rare. Remove the steaks from the pan.

Add the butter to the pan and let it sizzle, scraping the pan to remove any sediment. Add the brandy and shake the pan for 1 minute. Return the steaks and any resting juices to the pan, and quickly turn them over a few times in the pan to lightly coat in the sauce.

4 SERVINGS

1 tablespoon light olive oil
4 salmon cutlets, about 200 g (7 oz) each
2 teaspoons sea salt
lemon cheeks, to serve

CELERIAC REMOULADE
1 tablespoon lemon juice
½ small head celeriac, about 300 g (10½ oz) peeled
60 g (2¼ oz/¼ cup) good-quality mayonnaise
2 teaspoons capers, rinsed, drained and finely chopped
2 teaspoons dijon mustard
2 tablespoons thick (double/heavy) cream
2 tablespoons torn flat-leaf (Italian) parsley

» grilled fish cutlets with remoulade

For the remoulade, pour the lemon juice into a bowl. Using the coarse holes on a cheese grater, grate the celeriac directly into the bowl with the lemon juice. Use your hands to toss the grated celeriac with the lemon juice, separating the strands. Set aside for 30 minutes so the celeriac softens. Add the mayonnaise, capers, mustard, cream and parsley, season to taste and combine well. Set aside while cooking the fish.

Using your hands, rub the oil over the fish and sprinkle one side of each of the cutlets with half the salt.

Preheat a chargrill to high. When cooking fish, it is best that the cooking surface is hot and not to turn the fish too early or it will stick and tear the flesh.

Add the fish, salted side down. Sprinkle the remaining salt on the fish and cook for 2 minutes. Turn over and cook for another 2 minutes or until cooked to your liking. Serve with the remoulade and lemon cheeks on the side.

4 SERVINGS

4 baby snapper, about 300 g (10½ oz) each
1 tablespoon sea salt flakes
3 lemons, halved
1 tablespoon light olive oil

whole snapper with lemon «

Make several diagonal slashes on both sides of the fish. Rub the sea salt all over the fish and into the cuts. Stand the fish on a wire rack for 15 minutes. Squeeze one of the lemons all over the fish.

Preheat a barbecue hotplate to high. Wait for the plate to be hot before adding the oil.

Place the lemons, cut side down, in one corner of the hotplate. Put the fish on the hotplate and cook for 5 minutes, without turning or moving the fish or the skin will tear. Use a large metal spatula to slide under the fish in one quick movement and turn over. Cook for another 4-5 minutes or until just done. Put the fish on a serving plate. By this time, the lemons should be golden and soft on the cut side. Remove and serve with the fish.

4 SERVINGS

4 fillet steaks, about 150 g (5½ oz) each,
   and 2.5 cm (1 in)-thick
4 thick slices white bread
3 cloves garlic, crushed
1 teaspoon dijon mustard
80 g (2¾ oz) butter
1 tablespoon light olive oil

MUSHROOM & WHISKY SAUCE
50 g (1¾ oz) butter
4 French shallots, thinly sliced
60 g (2¼ oz/1 cup) thinly sliced Swiss
   brown mushrooms
1 beef stock cube, crumbled
40 ml (1¼ fl oz) whisky
60 ml (2 fl oz/¼ cup) pouring (whipping) cream
2 teaspoons lemon juice
1 tablespoon finely chopped flat-leaf
   (Italian) parsley

» fillet steaks with mushroom & whisky sauce

Season both sides of the steaks well with sea salt and freshly ground black pepper. Place on a wire rack and stand at room temperature for 1 hour.

For the mushroom and whisky sauce, melt the butter in a frying pan over high heat. Add the shallots and cook for 2–3 minutes or until softened. Add the mushrooms and cook for 5 minutes, stirring often until tender. Sprinkle the stock cube into the pan and stir to combine. Add the whisky and cook for 1 minute, then add 125 ml (4 fl oz/½ cup) of water and boil for 1 minute. Stir through the cream, lemon juice and parsley and bring to the boil. Cook for 2–3 minutes or until thickened, season to taste and set aside.

Preheat the oven to 180°C (350°F/Gas 4).

Using a biscuit cutter or a glass, cut out 8 cm (3¼ in) rounds from each slice of bread.

Place the garlic, mustard and half the butter in a small saucepan and cook over low heat until the butter has just melted. Remove from the heat, stir to combine, then brush the butter on one side of each of the bread rounds.

Heat the oil and remaining butter in a large frying pan over high heat. When the butter is sizzling and almost smoking hot, but not burnt, add the steaks and cook for 3 minutes on each side. Put the steaks on an oven tray. Put the bread rounds on the baking tray also and bake for 5 minutes or until the toast is just golden.

Remove from the oven and sit a steak on each of the toasts. Reheat the sauce over low heat, then pour over the steaks and serve.

Grilled food in restaurants often tastes good because it has been well seasoned. Just a generous sprinkling of sea salt and pepper a few minutes prior to cooking is all that's required. Possibly the most important rule to remember is to allow the meat time to rest. Heating causes meat to shrink or contract as the fibres tighten up. That great fillet steak hot off the grill will not only be more difficult to cut but chewy. Take it easy and let it rest for a more tender result.

6 cloves garlic, left whole and unpeeled
75 g (2½ oz) unsalted butter, softened
4 fillet steaks, about 200 g (7 oz) each
    and about 2 cm (¾ in) thick
4 rashers streaky bacon
1 tablespoon light olive oil

fillet mignon with roast « garlic butter

Preheat the oven to 220°C (425°F/Gas 7).

Wrap the garlic cloves in a piece of foil, place on an oven tray and bake for 20 minutes or until the cloves are soft when squeezed. Allow to cool. Once cooled, peel, then mash and combine well in a bowl with the softened butter. Set aside or refrigerate until needed.

Meanwhile, gently pound each steak so they are an even 1.5 cm (⅝ in) thickness all over. Season with sea salt and freshly ground black pepper and wrap a piece of streaky bacon around the centre of each steak, tucking in the ends to secure. Set aside for 30 minutes.

Heat a chargrill or barbecue flat plate to high. Lightly brush the steaks with oil and cook for 3 minutes on each side for rare. Remove and rest for 5 minutes.

While the steaks are resting, place the garlic butter in a small frying pan over medium heat and cook for 1 minute or until the garlic is sizzling. Transfer the steaks to a serving plate and pour over the hot butter.

4 SERVINGS

2 teaspoons sea salt
4 blue eye cod fillets, about 180 g (6½ oz)
    each, skin on
1 tablespoon light olive oil
lime cheeks and coriander (cilantro)
    sprigs, to serve

CURRY BUTTER
125 g (4½ oz) unsalted butter, room temperature
1 teaspoon finely grated ginger
1 clove garlic, crushed
2 tablespoons finely chopped spring onion
½ teaspoon ground cumin seeds
¼ teaspoon ground coriander seeds
¼ teaspoon ground fennel seeds
¼ teaspoon ground turmeric
¼ teaspoon sea salt

» blue eye with curry butter

For the curry butter, heat 40 g (1½ oz) butter in a frying pan over high heat. When sizzling but not burnt, add the ginger, garlic and spring onions and stir for 2-3 minutes or until the spring onions have softened. Stir in the spices and cook for another minute or until the mixture is aromatic. Add the salt then remove from the heat and cool to room temperature. Place the mixture in a bowl with the remaining butter and stir until well combined. Place a piece of plastic wrap on a work bench and spoon the butter down the centre, then roll up to make a log. Twist the ends to seal and refrigerate until needed. This can be made a day in advance.

Sprinkle the sea salt on the skin of the fish fillets.

Preheat a barbecue flat plate to high. When smoking hot, add the oil and use a metal spatula to spread the oil evenly over the surface of the flat plate. Cook the fish, skin side down, for 3-4 minutes, without moving or turning the fish for a crisp skin. When the skin is crisp and golden the fish can be easily flipped over without tearing the skin. Turn the fish over and cook for another 2 minutes.

Place the fish, skin side up on serving plates, top with slices of the curry butter and serve with the lime cheeks and coriander sprigs on the side.

4 SERVINGS

1 kg (2 lb 4 oz) calves' liver
2 tablespoons olive oil
4 cloves garlic, roughly chopped
1 tablespoon lemon juice
handful flat-leaf (Italian) parsley leaves, roughly chopped
grilled garlic toasts and lemon wedges, to serve

» seared calves' liver

Peel the membrane off the liver and discard. Trim the liver of any connecting fatty tissue or tubes and discard. Cut the liver crossways into 2 cm (¾ in) thick steak-like pieces.

Place the liver in a non-metallic dish with the oil and garlic. Season to taste with sea salt and freshly ground black pepper, turn to coat and set aside for 30 minutes.

Heat a barbecue hot plate to high. When smoking hot, add the liver slices and cook for 2–3 minutes. Turn over and cook for 2 minutes. Pour the lemon juice over the liver, letting it sizzle on the hot plate, then quickly turn the liver once more to coat in the juices. Transfer to a plate and sprinkle over the parsley. Serve with grilled garlic toasts and lemon wedges on the side.

12 cloves garlic, left whole and unpeeled
80 ml (2½ fl oz/⅓ cup) olive oil
1 tablespoon finely chopped rosemary
1 teaspoon finely grated lemon zest
60 ml (2 fl oz/¼ cup) lemon juice
1 teaspoon sea salt flakes, plus extra,
   for sprinkling
2 free-range chickens, about 1.5 kg (3 lb 5 oz)
   each, spatchcocked

spatchcocked chicken with «
rosemary & garlic

Peel and finely chop 4 cloves of garlic and place in a small saucepan with the olive oil over medium heat. When the garlic starts to sizzle, add the rosemary and lemon zest and cook for 2 minutes or until the rosemary is aromatic. Remove from the heat and allow to cool. Pour the oil through a fine sieve placed over a bowl, pressing to extract as much oil as possible. Stir the lemon juice into the oil and set aside. Transfer the solids to a small bowl, add the salt and ¼ teaspoon freshly ground black pepper and combine well.

Spread the garlic salt mixture all over the chicken skin, rubbing some under the breast skin. Set aside for 30 minutes.

Lightly crush the remaining unpeeled garlic with the flat side of a knife.

Preheat a chargrill to high.

When smoking hot, place the chickens on the grill, skin side down, reduce the heat to low and cook for 15 minutes, ensuring the chicken sizzles constantly on the hot plate, using a metal spatula to press down firmly on the chickens every 5 minutes or so. Turn the chickens over. Scatter the whole garlic cloves on and around the chicken and cook for another 10 minutes, again pressing down with the metal spatula. Turn the chickens over. Quickly stir the olive oil and lemon mixture and brush on the skin side of the chickens. Turn over again and cook for just a minute. Remove and cover loosely with foil to rest for 10–15 minutes before serving.

4 SERVINGS

4 pieces ocean trout fillet, about 180 g (6½ oz) each,
   skin on, pin-boned
2 teaspoons sea salt
60 ml (2 fl oz/¼ cup) light olive oil
lemon, halved, and radicchio wedges, to serve

» crispy-skinned trout

Preheat the oven to 220°C (425°F/Gas 7).

Rinse the trout, then pat dry well with paper towel and place, skin side up on a wire rack. Sprinkle the sea salt evenly over the skin and set aside for 15 minutes.

Heat a large ovenproof frying pan over high heat. Add the oil and, when almost smoking hot, carefully put the fish in the pan, skin side down. Cook for 3 minutes without turning or moving the fish. This will cause the pan to smoke and it may seem like the fish skin is burning yet it won't be.

Using large tongs, carefully remove the fish from the pan and pour off all but about 1 teaspoon of the hot oil. Return the fish to the pan, skin side up this time, and place the frying pan in the oven for 3 minutes or until the flesh is cooked to medium-rare. Stand for 5 minutes, then serve with lemon and radicchio wedges if desired.

4 tuna steaks, about 150–180 g (5½–6½ oz) each
60 ml (2 fl oz/¼ cup) olive oil
4 bay leaves
1 lemon, thinly sliced

CAPER MAYONNAISE
2 egg yolks, at room temperature
1 teaspoon dijon mustard
2 teaspoons lemon juice
125 ml (4 fl oz/½ cup) light olive oil
1 tablespoon small capers in salt, well rinsed,
    drained and roughly chopped
1 tablespoon finely chopped chervil, plus extra
    chervil sprigs, to serve

grilled tuna with « caper mayonnaise

Place the tuna in a non-metallic dish with the olive oil, bay leaves and lemon. Cover and set aside for 30 minutes.

Meanwhile, for the caper mayonnaise, place the egg yolks, mustard, lemon juice and a pinch of sea salt in a small bowl. Wet a dish cloth and fold up into a square on a work bench. Sit the bowl on top. This will allow you to use both hands to whisk and add oil at the same time without the bowl moving too much. Or have someone hold the bowl for you. Start to whisk the egg yolk mixture and as you do, add a thin steady stream of the oil. Keep whisking and adding the oil until all the oil has been added and the mixture is thick and emulsified. Stir through the capers and

chervil and check the seasoning. Transfer to a serving bowl, cover closely with plastic wrap and refrigerate until needed. This can be made several hours ahead.

To cook the tuna, preheat a chargrill to high. Shake off excess oil from the tuna, reserving the bay leaves and lemon. When smoking hot, cook the tuna for 2 minutes on each side. Transfer to a serving plate. Add the bay leaves and lemon slices to the grill and cook for a minute or until charred.

Serve the tuna garnished with the grilled bay leaf, lemon and extra chervil sprigs with the caper mayonnaise on the side.

4 SERVINGS

40 g (1½ oz) butter
1 small onion, finely chopped
1 clove garlic, crushed
2 rashers streaky bacon, rind removed,
    finely chopped
500 g (1 lb 2 oz) minced (ground) beef
60 ml (2 fl oz/¼ cup) stout beer
1 egg, lightly beaten
light olive oil, for drizzling
toasted burger buns, shredded lettuce, sliced
    tomato, crispy bacon, sliced beetroot and
    cheddar cheese and barbecue sauce, to serve

» stout beef burgers

Melt the butter in a small frying pan over medium heat. Add the onion, garlic and bacon and cook for 2-3 minutes or until soft. Transfer to a bowl, cool slightly, then add the beef and beer and season to taste. Using your hands, combine well, then cover and refrigerate for a few hours, so the beer flavours the beef.

Add the egg to the beef and combine with your hands. Divide the mixture into 4 equal portions then shape into patties. Place on a plate, cover and refrigerate until needed. The patties can be made up to one day in advance.

Remove the patties from the refrigerator 30 minutes before cooking.

Preheat a barbecue flat plate to high and drizzle with a little olive oil. Cook the patties for 5 minutes on each side or until well cooked on the outside. They may still be slightly pink in the centre. Cook for an extra 2 minutes each side to cook all the way through if desired. Serve with the toasted buns, salad, bacon, cheese and sauce.

3 large pork fillets, about 400 g (14 oz) each
2 tablespoons light olive oil

MUSTARD CREAM SAUCE
40 g (1½ oz) butter
1 tablespoon plain (all-purpose) flour
125 ml (4 fl oz/½ cup) veal or beef stock
125 ml (4 fl oz/½ cup) cream
2 teaspoons wholegrain mustard
2 tablespoons brandy

pork skewers with «
mustard cream sauce

Cut the pork into large bite-sized pieces and toss in a bowl with the olive oil. Set aside.

For the mustard cream sauce, melt the butter in a small saucepan over medium heat. Stir in the flour and cook for 1 minute, then remove from the heat and stir in the stock. Whisk over medium heat for 1 minute or until thickened. Add the cream and mustard and stir until smooth. Season to taste and set aside while cooking the pork.

Preheat a chargrill to high.

Thread the meat evenly onto 8 large metal skewers. Season the pork well and cook on the grill for 12 minutes, cooking each of the sides for about 4 minutes. You may need to cook in batches.

Gently reheat the sauce over low heat. Serve a skewer with the sauce on the side. Or remove the meat from the skewer and spoon the sauce over. Serve with cos lettuce wedges.

2 SERVINGS

1 large cooked lobster, about 1 kg (2 lb 4 oz)
250 ml (9 fl oz/1 cup) milk
1 small onion, chopped
2 cloves
1 bay leaf
50 g (1¾ oz) butter
2 French shallots, finely chopped
2 tablespoons plain (all-purpose) flour
125 ml (4 fl oz/½ cup) white wine
250 ml (9 fl oz/1 cup) pouring (whipping) cream
1 teaspoon dijon mustard
100 g (3½ oz) gruyère cheese, grated

» lobster thermidor

Have the fishmonger split the whole lobster down the centre. Remove the meat from the lobster and chop into large bite-sized pieces. Reserve the meat and place the shells on a oven tray.

Place the milk, onion, cloves and bay leaf in a saucepan and bring to the boil. Remove from the heat and allow to cool. Strain through a fine sieve, discard the solids and reserve the milk.

Heat the butter in a saucepan over high heat. When the butter is sizzling, add the shallots and stir for 1 minute or until just soft. Stir in the flour to make a thick paste. Add the wine and stir until smooth. Add the reserved milk, cream, mustard and half the cheese. Reduce the heat to low heat and stir for 4–5 minutes or until thick and smooth. Remove from the heat, then add the lobster meat and combine well.

Spoon the mixture into the lobster shells and sprinkle the remaining cheese on top. Cook under a hot grill (broiler) for 5 minutes or until the cheese sauce is golden and bubbling.

baked 115

Some recipes stand the ultimate test of time. For something to be considered both retro and stylish at the same time is the greatest test of all. Some of these recipes may very well have been in your parents' repertoire, saved for those special occasions: veal parmigiana, beef burgundy or a rack of lamb. Of course this depends entirely on your parents' prowess and confidence in the kitchen! And others were left well and truly for dining out: beef Wellington, lobster thermidor and surely the chateaubriand for two. But this isn't all fancy pants and poshed up ... pies are as about as unpretentious as you can get and there are several great ones to choose from in this chapter.

4 SERVINGS

4 small chickens, about 600 g (1 lb 5 oz) each
125 g (4½ oz) butter, softened to room temperature
250 ml (9 fl oz/1 cup) chicken stock

» chicken in a basket

Preheat the oven to 180°C (350°F/Gas 4).

Rinse and pat dry the chickens. Tie the legs together with kitchen string. Rub the butter all over the skin on the top side of the chickens and season with sea salt and freshly ground black pepper. Place in a large roasting pan, making sure they are not touching. Set aside for 30 minutes.

Pour the stock into the pan around the chickens, then roast for 1 hour or until the skin is golden, basting the chickens every 20 minutes.

Sit each chicken on several layers of paper towel for 5 minutes to rest. Transfer to individual baskets, sprinkle with sea salt and serve with finger bowls, another bowl for bones and lots of napkins.

500 ml (17 fl oz/2 cups) light olive oil
1 onion, chopped
1 clove garlic, finely chopped
400 g (14 oz) tin chopped tomatoes
½ teaspoon dried oregano
75 g (2½ oz/½ cup) plain (all-purpose) flour, seasoned

250 g (9 oz) stale breadcrumbs (such as ciabatta)
2 eggs
4 veal schnitzels, about 150 g (5½ oz) each
150 g (5½ oz) mozzarella cheese, thinly sliced
50 g (1¾ oz) finely grated parmesan cheese
lemon wedges, to serve

veal parmigiana «

Heat 1 tablespoon of the oil in a saucepan over high heat. Cook the onion and garlic for 2–3 minutes or until soft. Add the tomatoes and oregano and cook for 5 minutes or until slightly thickened. Season to taste and set aside.

Preheat the oven to 200°C (400°F/Gas 6).

Place the flour and breadcrumbs on separate plates. Place the eggs and 1 tablespoon of the oil in a shallow bowl and lightly beat.

Dust the schnitzels in the flour to lightly coat. Dip in the egg mixture, allowing the excess to drain, then coat in the breadcrumbs.

Heat the remaining oil in a large frying pan over high heat. When the surface of the oil is shimmering, add two of the schnitzels and cook for 2–3 minutes each side, shaking the pan gently, until the crumbs are golden. Drain on paper towel, then repeat with the remaining schnitzels.

Place the schnitzels in a single layer in a large baking dish. Spoon over the tomato sauce, then top with slices of mozzarella and sprinkle with the parmesan. Bake for 10 minutes or until the cheese is golden and melted. Serve with lemon wedges.

6 SERVINGS

40 g (1½ oz) butter
900 g (2 lb) onions, thinly sliced
2 bay leaves
375 ml (13 fl oz/1½ cups) fish stock
750 ml (26 fl oz/3 cups) cream
2 teaspoons mustard powder
750 g (1 lb 10 oz) smoked cod or haddock, skin and bones discarded
2 sheets pre-rolled puff pastry
1 tablespoon milk

» creamy smoked fish pie

Heat the butter in a heavy-based saucepan over medium heat. Add the onion and bay leaves and stir well to break up the onion. Cover and cook, stirring often to prevent the onion from catching, for 30 minutes or until soft. Remove the lid and increase the heat to high. Cook, stirring often for another 8–9 minutes, until the onions turn a pale caramel colour. Add the stock and simmer until reduced by half. Reduce the heat to medium, add the cream and mustard and cook for 15 minutes, stirring frequently with a large wooden spoon — be careful as the mixture will be very hot and bubbling. Remove from the heat and cool. Remove the bay leaves, season to taste and process in a food processor until smooth.

Preheat the oven to 220°C (425°F/Gas 7). Cut the fish into large bite-sized pieces. Divide half the onion mixture among six 10 cm (4 in) round ramekins or pie dishes. Divide the fish among the ramekins and spoon over the remaining onion mixture.

Cut six 12 cm (4½ in) circles from the puff pastry. Cover each pie with a circle of pastry and press around the edges with a fork to seal. Use a small sharp knife to make 2–3 incisions in the pastry to allow the steam to escape. Brush the tops with a little milk, place on an oven tray and bake for 20–25 minutes until golden and puffed.

4 SERVINGS

4 individual lamb racks, each with 3 cutlets
1 tablespoon light olive oil
50 g (1¾ oz) butter, softened to room temperature
1 tablespoon dijon mustard
100 g (3½ oz/1 cup) stale breadcrumbs
1 clove garlic, crushed
2 tablespoons finely chopped flat-leaf (Italian) parsley
2 tablespoons finely chopped basil leaves
½ teaspoon dried oregano

» rack of lamb with herb crust

Season the fat side of each of the racks with sea salt and ground black pepper to taste.

Heat the oil in a large heavy-based frying pan over high heat. When smoking, place two of the lamb racks in the pan, skin side down, and cook for 2 minutes. Remove and cook the other two racks. Sit the racks on a chopping board, skin side up, and allow to cool to room temperature.

Preheat the oven to 180°C (350°F/Gas 4).

Place the butter, mustard, breadcrumbs, garlic and herbs in a bowl and use your hands to mix together. Smear the mixture all over the browned side of the lamb racks. Place, crust side up, in a roasting pan and bake for 20 minutes or until the crust is golden.

500 g (1 lb 2 oz) mixed mushrooms (such as
    Swiss brown, button and cap)
80 g (2¾ oz) butter
1 teaspoon finely chopped thyme leaves
1 clove garlic, finely chopped
400 g (14 oz) skinless chicken thigh fillets, cut
    into large bite-sized pieces

1 leek, white part only, halved lengthways
35 g (1¼ oz/¼ cup) plain (all-purpose) flour
250 ml (9 fl oz/1 cup) chicken stock
250 ml (9 fl oz/1 cup) cream
5 g (⅛ oz/¼ cup) roughly chopped flat-leaf
    (Italian) parsley
1 sheet ready-rolled puff pastry
1 egg, lightly beaten

chicken & mushroom « pot pie

Trim the stems from the mushrooms and discard. Roughly chop any larger caps, leaving the button mushrooms whole.

Heat half the butter in a large frying pan over high heat. When sizzling, add the mushrooms, thyme and garlic and cook, shaking the pan, for 5 minutes or until the mushrooms soften and start to brown. Remove from the pan.

Add the remaining butter to the pan. When sizzling, add half the chicken and cook for 2–3 minutes or until golden all over. Using a slotted spoon, remove the chicken from the pan, leaving the hot fat in the pan to reheat. Repeat with the remaining chicken and remove from the pan.

Reduce the heat to medium. Add the leek to the pan and stir, scraping the bottom of the pan to remove any sediment, for 2–3 minutes or until the leek has softened. Return the mushrooms and chicken to the pan and stir for 2–3 minutes. Sprinkle the flour into the pan and stir for 2 minutes or until all the ingredients begin to come together. Gradually add the stock, stirring until thick and well combined. Stir in the cream and parsley, reduce the heat to low and cook for 2–3 minutes or until thickened. Season to taste and spoon into four 375 ml (13 fl oz/1½ cup) capacity pie dishes or ramekins. Allow to cool.

Preheat the oven to 220°C (425°F/Gas 7).

From the pastry, cut out 4 lids slightly larger than the dish. Brush a little beaten egg around the rim of the pie dishes and lay the pastry on top, pressing onto the dish to seal. Brush the top with egg, place on an oven tray and bake for 23–30 minutes or until the pastry is golden and puffed.

50 g (1¾ oz) butter
150 g (5½ oz) French shallots, roughly chopped
250 g (9 oz) field mushrooms, roughly chopped
125 ml (4 fl oz/1 cup) white wine
7 g (⅛ oz/¼ cup) roughly chopped flat-leaf
    (Italian) parsley
700 g (1 lb 9 oz) beef fillet in one piece

1 tablespoon light olive oil
1 egg, lightly beaten
2 teaspoons sea salt flakes
wholegrain mustard, to serve

PASTRY
250 g (9 oz/1⅔ cups) plain (all-purpose) flour
150 g (5½ oz) cold unsalted butter, chopped
2 egg yolks

beef wellington «

For the pastry, place the flour and butter in the bowl of a food processor and sit in the freezer for 10 minutes or until chilled. Pulse the ingredients a few times to just combine. With the motor running, add the egg yolks and just enough iced water, about 2–3 tablespoons, to wet the dry ingredients enough that they are on the verge of coming together. Do not overwork or the pastry will toughen and shrink when cooked. Shape into a disc. Wrap in plastic wrap and refrigerate for 30 minutes.

Melt the butter in a large frying pan over high heat and cook the shallots for 5 minutes or until golden. Add the mushrooms and stir for 2–3 minutes or until softened. Add the wine and cook until almost evaporated, then stir in the parsley and season well. Remove from the heat and cool for 10 minutes. Place the mixture in a food processor and process until smooth, then transfer to a bowl and refrigerate until needed.

Season the beef well. Heat the olive oil in a frying pan over high heat. When smoking hot, add the beef and cook for 4–5 minutes, turning often

so it is evenly browned all over. Remove from the pan and allow to cool to room temperature.

Preheat the oven to 220°C (425°F/Gas 7) and line a baking tray with baking paper.

Roll the pastry between two sheets of baking paper until it is 2–3 mm (1⁄16 – ⅛ in) thick and forms a 20 x 30 cm (8 x 12 in) rectangle. Neaten the edges and reserve the trimmings. Peel off the top layer of baking paper, then turn the pastry so that there is one long edge facing you. Spread the mushroom mixture all over the pastry, leaving a 3–4 cm (1¼–1½ in) border around the entire edge. Lay the beef fillet lengthways on the bottom of the pastry. Use the bottom layer of baking paper to roll the beef over, tuck in the sides of the pastry and continue to roll until the beef is entirely enclosed in the pastry. Place the beef, seam side down, on the baking tray. Decorate the top with the pastry trimmings if desired, then brush all over with the beaten egg, sprinkle with the sea salt and bake for 30–35 minutes or until the pastry is golden and crisp. Allow to cool for 10 minutes before slicing.

4 SERVINGS

2 kg (4 lb 8 oz) beef short ribs
1 teaspoon chilli powder
2 teaspoons sea salt
1 teaspoon freshly ground black pepper

BARBECUE SAUCE
40 g (1½ oz) unsalted butter
1 small onion, finely chopped
2 cloves garlic, crushed
1 teaspoon chilli powder
125 ml (4 fl oz/½ cup) white vinegar

125 ml (4 fl oz/½ cup) tomato passata
  (puréed tomatoes)
1 tablespoon Worcestershire sauce
1 teaspoon mustard powder
1 teaspoon smoked paprika
2 tablespoons treacle
lemon wedges, to serve

» slow cooked beef ribs with real barbecue sauce

Cut the ribs into portions of 3-4 bones each and place on a tray. Combine the chilli powder, salt and pepper in a bowl and rub all over the ribs. Set aside for 1 hour.

Meanwhile, for the barbecue sauce, melt the butter in a small saucepan over high heat. Add the onion and garlic and cook for 2-3 minutes or until the onion is soft. Add the chilli powder and cook for a few seconds or until aromatic. Add the remaining ingredients and bring to the boil. Reduce the heat to low-medium heat and simmer for 4-5 minutes or until dark and syrupy. Allow to cool then transfer to a food processor. Process until smooth. Set aside.

Preheat the oven to 160°C (315°F/Gas 2-3).

Sit the ribs on a baking rack set over a baking tray half filled with water. Bake for 2 hours, topping up the water if needs be. After 2 hours, increase the oven temperature to 200°C (400°F/Gas 6), start brushing the beef with the barbecue sauce, avoiding the bones, every 5 minutes for 20 minutes until the ribs are sticky and dark. Serve with lemon wedges.

2 SERVINGS

500 g (1 lb 2 oz) centre cut beef eye fillet
1 tablespoon olive oil
1 teaspoon fine sea salt

SAUCE CHATEAUBRIAND
2 tablespoons finely chopped French shallots
2 small sprigs thyme
1 bay leaf
125 ml (4 fl oz/½ cup) white wine

500 ml (17 fl oz/2 cups) veal or beef stock
40 g (1½ oz) unsalted butter, softened to
    room temperature
1 tablespoon plain (all-purpose) flour
1 tablespoon finely chopped flat-leaf
    (Italian) parsley
1 teaspoon lemon juice
1 tablespoon finely chopped tarragon

chateaubriand for two «

Rub the beef all over with the oil, then the salt. Sit on a rack a set aside for 1 hour.

Meanwhile, for the sauce, place the shallots, thyme, bay leaf and wine into a saucepan and cook over medium heat until there is only about 1 tablespoon liquid remaining. Add the stock and simmer until reduced to about 125 ml (4 fl oz/½ cup). Strain the sauce through a fine sieve, discard the solids and return the liquid to a clean pan.

Combine the butter and flour thoroughly in a bowl. Add the parsley and lemon juice and mix to a smooth paste.

Heat the sauce over medium heat until it comes to the simmer. Reduce the heat to low. Whisking continuously, add 1 tablespoon of butter mixture at a time to the sauce. Remove from the heat.

Preheat the oven to 220°C (425°F/Gas 7).

Place the beef in a roasting pan and cook for 10 minutes. Turn over and cook for another 10 minutes. Remove from the oven, cover loosely with foil and rest for 10 minutes. Pour any of the resting juices into the sauce, add the tarragon and season to taste. Stir over low heat for 2–3 minutes or until just hot. Thickly slice the beef and serve with the sauce.

4 SERVINGS

1 kg (2 lb 4 oz) chuck steak, trimmed and cut
    into large bite-sized pieces
750 ml (26 fl oz/3 cups) red wine
1 carrot, chopped
1 onion, chopped
1 celery stalk, chopped
6 cloves garlic, roughly smashed
2 sprigs thyme
2 bay leaves
35 g (1¼ oz/¼ cup) plain (all-purpose) flour
2 tablespoons olive oil
50 g (1¾ oz) butter

100 g (3½ oz) streaky bacon, sliced
    into 1.5 cm (⅝ in) batons
12 small pickling onions, peeled
24 button mushrooms
60 ml (2 fl oz/¼ cup) brandy
1 beef stock cube
2 teaspoons lemon juice
handful flat-leaf (Italian) parsley leaves,
    finely chopped
rum and maple mashed sweet potato, to serve
    (see page 176)

» beef burgundy

Place the steak in a large bowl with the wine, carrot, chopped onion, celery, garlic, thyme and bay leaves. Combine well then cover and refrigerate overnight, mixing often.

Pour the mixture into a fine sieve placed over a saucepan. Pick out and set aside the meat pieces. Tip the other solids back into the liquid in the saucepan and bring to the boil over high heat. Reduce the heat to medium and simmer for 30 minutes or until the wine has reduced by about half. Strain through a fine sieve, discard the solids and reserve the liquid.

Preheat the oven to 150°C (300°F/Gas 2).

Place the flour on a plate and season to taste with sea salt and freshly ground black pepper. Roll each piece of meat in the flour to lightly coat. Heat the oil and butter in a heavy-based casserole dish over medium heat. Add the bacon and cook for 8–10 minutes until really well browned and crisp.

Remove from the pan, leaving as much fat in the pan as possible. Cook the beef in batches, until browned all over, placing the browned beef in a bowl as you go.

Add the pickling onions to the pan and stir for 4–5 minutes or until golden. Remove the onions and add to the beef. Add the mushrooms to the pan and cook for 4–5 minutes or until softened and golden. Remove from the pan. Add the brandy and cook for 1 minute, scraping the base of the pan to remove any sediment. Return the bacon, beef, onions and mushrooms to the pan, and tip in any juices from the bowl. Add the reserved wine mixture and bring to the boil. Crumble the stock cube into the pan, stir to combine. Cover and transfer to the oven. Bake for 2 hours or until the meat is very tender, stirring after 1 hour. Stir through the lemon juice and parsley, season to taste and serve with mashed sweet potato.

1 kg (2 lb 4 oz) pork belly, skin on
1 tablespoon fine sea salt
1 tablespoon light olive oil
2 teaspoons sea salt flakes
½ teaspoon fennel seeds

APPLE SAUCE
4 tart cooking apples, such as granny smith
55 g (1¾ oz/¼ cup) white sugar
¼ teaspoon Chinese five-spice powder

crispy pork belly with « apple sauce

Cut the pork into four equal sized portions. Rinse well and pat dry. Sit the pork in a oven tray, side by side, and cover with baking paper. Sit a flat, heavy object on top and refrigerate overnight.

Remove the pork from the refrigerator, rinse well and pat dry. Rub the fine sea salt all over the skin and sides of the pork and set aside for 1 hour.

Preheat the oven to 150°C (300°F/Gas 2).

Rinse the salt off the pork pieces and again pat dry. Brush the skin with some of the oil and pour the remainder in a oven tray. Sprinkle the sea salt flakes and fennel seeds on the skin of the pork. Place in the baking tray, skin side up, and bake for 3 hours, lightly basting every hour. Increase the heat to 240°C (475°F/Gas 8) and cook for another 5-10 minutes, keeping your eye on the skin, until it is golden and very crisp. Remove from the oven and rest for 10 minutes before serving.

Meanwhile, for the apple sauce, peel, core and roughly chop the apples. Place in a heavy-based saucepan with the sugar, five-spice powder and 125 ml (4 fl oz/½ cup) of water. Cover and cook over medium heat for 10-15 minutes, stirring often until they are completely soft and mushy. Use a potato masher to roughly mash the apples, leaving smaller chunks of apple in the sauce. Serve with the hot crisp pork belly.

Pork belly is no longer really that hard to find. If you live near a Chinese butcher, all good. Just buy some boneless pork belly that is used in slow-braised Chinese recipes. It is usually sold as one long, narrow piece, which is perfect. Just cut it crossways into the portion size you want. Weighing it down is a restaurant trick that will give a you a very professional looking end result. I have not fussed here with too many flavourings ... just the one, in fact. I am using fennel but a little caraway would be nice too. Just serve up with a good apple sauce and some sort of mashed root veggie on the side.

BEETROOT AND APPLE PUDDING
140 g (5 oz/1 cup) grated beetroot
40 g (1½ oz) butter
2 tablespoons olive oil
1 small onion, finely chopped

4 pork hocks
1 tablespoon light olive oil
1 teaspoon caraway seeds
1 teaspoon sea salt

2 cloves garlic, finely chopped
200 g (7 oz/1 cup) grated green apple
60 g (2¼ oz/½ cup) seedless raisins
1 tablespoon white wine vinegar
1 tablespoon soft brown sugar
100 g (3½ oz/1 cup) stale breadcrumbs
1 egg, lightly beaten
185 ml (6 fl oz/¾ cup) chicken stock

roast pork hocks with « beetroot & apple pudding

Preheat the oven to 160°C (315°F/Gas 2–3).

Rub the pork hocks all over with the oil, caraway seeds and sea salt. Place in a roasting pan, cover with foil and roast for 3 hours. Remove the foil and increase the oven temperature to 240°C (475°F/Gas 8). Roast for another 15–20 minutes or until the skin is golden and very crisp, and the meat is falling off the bones. Remove from the oven, reduce the oven temperature to 180°C (350°F/Gas 4) and cover the hocks loosely with foil.

Meanwhile, for the beetroot and apple pudding, cook the grated beetroot in boiling water for 2 minutes. Drain well. Heat the butter and oil in a small frying pan over medium heat and cook the onion and garlic for 5–6 minutes or until soft. Place in a bowl with the beetroot, apple, raisins, vinegar, brown sugar, breadcrumbs, egg and stock, season to taste and set aside.

Once the hocks have come out of the oven and the oven has come down in temperature, pour the pudding mixture into a lightly greased 1 litre (35 fl oz/4 cup) capacity ceramic baking dish and bake for 35–40 minutes.

Serve the warm hocks with the beetroot and apple pudding to the side.

4 SERVINGS

800 g (1 lb 12 oz) chuck steak, cut into bite-sized pieces
75 g (2½ oz/½ cup) plain (all-purpose) flour
500 g (1 lb 2 oz) prepared (trimmed) veal kidneys, cut into bite-sized pieces
150 g (5½ oz) butter
3 onions, thinly sliced
400 ml (14 fl oz) beef or veal stock
2 sheets good-quality frozen shortcrust pastry
1 egg yolk, beaten with 2 teaspoons water

» steak & kidney pies

Place the beef pieces in a sieve with half the flour and season well. Toss the beef to coat in the flour, allowing any excess flour to fall through the sieve. Place the beef on a plate. Repeat with the kidneys, using the remaining flour.

Heat 50 g (1¾ oz) butter in a heavy-based saucepan over high heat. When the butter is sizzling, add the onion and stir to coat well. Reduce the heat to medium, cover and cook for 8–10 minutes, or until softened and lightly golden, stirring from time to time so the onions do not catch on the bottom of the pan. Transfer to a bowl.

Add another 50 g (1¾ oz) butter to the pan and place over medium-high heat. When the butter is sizzling, cook the steak and kidneys in batches, without overcrowding the pan, until browned on all sides. You will need to add the remaining butter while browning off the last few

batches. Return the onions, meat and kidneys to the pan with the stock. Bring to the boil, stirring to combine and to remove any sediment from the base of the pan. Reduce the heat to low, cover and simmer gently for 1 hour, stirring from time to time. Increase the heat to high, uncover and boil for 10 minutes or until thickened. Season well.

Spoon the mixture into four 310–375 ml (10¾ –13 fl oz/1¼- 1½ cup) capacity pie dishes or ramekins and allow to cool to room temperature.

Preheat the oven to 180°C (350°F/Gas 4).

Cut out four pastry pieces, slightly larger than the tops of the pie dishes. Fold or press to seal around the edges and brush all over with the beaten egg. Sprinkle with sea salt. Place on an oven tray and bake for 30–35 minutes or until the pastry is golden.

60 ml (2 fl oz/¼ cup) olive oil
4 lamb shanks
1 onion, chopped
1 clove garlic, chopped
2 sprigs thyme
400 g (14 oz) tin chopped tomatoes
250 ml (9 fl oz/1 cup) beef stock
250 ml (9 fl oz/1 cup) red wine
100 g (3½ oz/½ cup) green lentils, washed
7 g (⅛ oz/¼ cup) roughly chopped flat-leaf
  (Italian) parsley

lamb shanks with red wine, « lentils & herbs

Preheat the oven to 160°C (315°F/Gas 2–3).

Heat 1 tablespoon of the oil in a heavy-based casserole dish over high heat. Cook 2 of the shanks for 4–5 minutes, turning often until well browned. Remove from the pan. Add another tablespoon of oil and the remaining lamb shanks. Cook until well browned, then remove from the pan.

Add the remaining oil to the pan and cook the onion, garlic and thyme for 2–3 minutes, scraping the bottom of the pan to remove sediment.

Return the shanks to the pan with all the remaining ingredients except the parsley. Bring to the boil and cover tightly, then transfer to the oven and bake for 2 hours, turning the shanks after 1 hour. Stir through the parsley, season to taste and serve.

4 SERVINGS

4 beef rib eyes on the bone, about 1.5–1.6 kg
   (3 lb 5 oz–3 lb 8 oz)
1 tablespoon sea salt flakes
2 teaspoons freshly ground black pepper
80 g (2¾ oz) unsalted butter
2 tablespoons light olive oil
12 small pickling onions, peeled
3 cloves garlic, finely chopped
handful flat-leaf (Italian) parsley leaves, finely chopped
mustard and crunchy roast potatoes with rosemary (see page 166), to serve

» standing beef roast with onions

Preheat the oven to 150°C (300°F/Gas 2).

Remove the beef from the refrigerator and place on a rack. Combine the salt and pepper in a small bowl and rub all over the beef. Set aside for 1 hour.

Heat half the butter and half the oil in a large heavy-based, ovenproof frying pan or roasting pan over high heat. When the pan is smoking hot, add the beef, top side down, and cook for 4–5 minutes without moving. Turn over and cook for another 5 minutes. Remove the meat from the pan and discard the hot fat in the pan.

Add the remaining butter and oil, swirling the pan around so the butter sizzles. Add the onions and garlic and toss to coat in the butter. Push the onions and garlic to the outside of the pan to make room for the beef, then place the beef in the centre, top side up. Place in the oven and roast for 1 hour for medium-rare, turning the onions from time to time.

Remove the beef from the pan and allow to rest in a warm place, uncovered, for 20–25 minutes. Add the parsley to the onions and stir to combine with the pan juices. Return the onions to the oven while the beef is resting.

Pour any resting juices into the onions, then cut between the ribs to give four pieces of meat with a bone in each. Spoon over the onions and serve with mustard and crunchy roast potatoes with rosemary.

4 SERVINGS

750 g (1 lb 10 oz) braising beef, cut into
   3 cm (1¼ in) pieces
35 g (1¼ oz/¼ cup) plain (all-purpose) flour
2 tablespoons light olive oil
50 g (1¾ oz) butter
2 onions, thinly sliced
1 carrot, finely diced
2 celery stalks, finely diced

1 small handful fresh herbs (sprigs rosemary,
   thyme, bay leaf)
250 ml (9 fl oz/1 cup) Guinness
250 ml (9 fl oz/1 cup) beef stock
1 teaspoon Worcestershire sauce
100 g (3½ oz) cheddar cheese, grated
2 sheets pre-rolled puff pastry
1 egg, lightly beaten

beef & guinness pie «

Place the beef and flour in a ziplock or plastic bag and season to taste with sea salt and freshly ground black pepper. Toss the bag so all the beef pieces are coated in the flour, then tip the beef into a bowl.

Heat half the oil and half the butter in a large heavy-based casserole dish over high heat. Add half the beef and cook for 4–5 minutes, turning the pieces often until browned all over. Remove from the pan and repeat with the remaining oil, butter and beef.

Add the onion, carrot and celery to the pan and stir for 4–5 minutes or until soft. Return the beef to the pan, then add the herbs, Guinness, stock and Worcestershire sauce and bring to the boil. Reduce the heat to low, cover and cook for 1½

hours or until the beef is tender, stirring every now and then to prevent the beef from catching on the base. Remove the lid, increase the heat to high and boil for 5 minutes or until the sauce has thickened. Remove from the heat, season to taste and cool.

Preheat the oven to 180°C (350°F/Gas 4).

Remove the bay leaves and any herb stalks from the beef mixture. Divide the mixture among four 375 ml (13 fl oz/1½ cup) capacity ramekins or pie dishes and sprinkle the cheese over the top.

From the pastry, cut out rounds, slightly larger than the ramekins or dishes, and place on top of each pie. Press, pleat or fold around the edges to seal. Brush the tops with the beaten egg, place on an oven tray and bake for 25–30 minutes, until the pastry is puffed and golden.

—sides

The side act is like a support for the main event but sometimes, can become a star in its own right. How often do we remember a really good chip? Too often, in my case. Besides the chip, potatoes abound in other forms: crunchy roasted potatoes with rosemary; potato gratin; garlicky mash and pan-fried rosti. From winter warming comfort food like cauliflower mornay and creamed leeks to simply cooked prime-season veggies spiked with fresh herbs; buttered zucchini and beans

with mint; mushrooms with tarragon, baked
mushrooms and tomatoes; corn on the
cob with butter. Who said these were sides?
You can of course turn back and see what mains
tickle your fancy or you could just cook a few
sausages, a great big t-bone or lamb cutlet on the
grill. These make great summer dishes too, serve
them up with a bacon, tomato and herb bake;
classic waldorf salad or my old-school favourite,
a tomato, onion and bread salad.

4 SERVINGS

4 large all-purpose potatoes, such as desiree
500 g (1 lb 2 oz) duck fat
sea salt flakes, to serve

thick-cut chips cooked « in duck fat

Peel and wash the potatoes. Cut the potatoes into 1–1.5 cm (½–⅝ in) thick chips.

Bring a large saucepan of water to the boil and cook the chips for 2 minutes. Drain well. Spread out on a clean tea towel and allow to cool.

Place the fat in a large frying pan over low -medium heat. Working in batches and, using kitchen tongs, add a handful of the chips and cook for 8–10 minutes, so they just gently simmer in the fat and do not brown. Use a slotted spoon to remove the chips and drain on paper towel.

Increase the heat to high. The fat is ready when the surface begins to shimmer. Again working in batches and using tongs, carefully add a handful of the chips to the hot oil. Cook for 2–3 minutes, until golden and crisp. Drain on paper towel, sprinkle with sea salt and serve immediately.

4 SERVINGS

225 g (8 oz) macaroni
100 g (3½ oz/1 cup) stale breadcrumbs
40 g (1½ oz) cold butter
chopped flat-leaf (Italian) parsley, to serve

CHEESE SAUCE
60 g (2¼ oz) butter
35 g (1¼ oz/¼ cup) plain (all-purpose) flour
375 ml (13 fl oz/1½ cups) milk
125 g (4½ oz/1 cup) grated cheddar cheese
1 teaspoon dijon mustard

» macaroni & cheese

For the cheese sauce, heat the butter in a saucepan over medium heat until is sizzling and melted. Add the flour and stir for 1 minute, then remove from the heat. Stirring continuously, gradually add the milk and then return to the heat and stir for 2–3 minutes or until thick and smooth. Add the cheese, and mustard and stir until melted and smooth. Remove from the heat and season to taste.

Preheat the oven to 220°C (425°F/Gas 7).

Cook the macaroni in boiling water for 8–10 minutes — it should still be firm to the bite. Drain well, then return to the pan, add the cheese sauce and combine well. Spoon into a 1.5 litre (52 fl oz/6 cup) baking dish. Combine the breadcrumbs and parsley and sprinkle over the macaroni. Grate the cold butter over the top, then bake for 15 minutes or until golden and bubbling. Serve sprinkled with chopped parsley leaves.

4 SERVINGS

85 g (3 oz) cold butter, chopped
1 tablespoon olive oil
2 rashers bacon, rind removed, finely chopped
1 onion, finely chopped
1 clove garlic, crushed
4 vine-ripened tomatoes, thinly sliced
40 g (1½ oz/½ cup) coarse fresh breadcrumbs
½ teaspoon dried oregano or Italian herbs

bacon, tomato & herb bake «

Preheat the oven to 180°C (350°F/Gas 4) and lightly grease a shallow 1 litre (35 fl oz/4 cup) capacity baking dish.

Heat 20 g (¾ oz) butter and the oil in a frying pan over high heat until the butter is sizzling. Add the bacon and cook for 4–5 minutes or until crisp. Add the onion and cook for 2–3 minutes or until soft. Stir through the garlic and then remove from the heat.

Lay one-quarter of the tomato slices on the bottom of the greased dish and spoon over one-quarter of the bacon mixture. Repeat the layering with the remaining tomatoes and bacon mixture, finishing with a layer of tomatoes.

Combine the breadcrumbs and dried herbs in a bowl and sprinkle over the tomatoes. Scatter the remaining chopped butter over the top and bake for 35–40 minutes or until golden and bubbling.

4 SERVINGS

6 medium desiree potatoes, peeled
60 ml (2 fl oz/¼ cup) extra virgin olive oil
2 sprigs rosemary
½ teaspoon sea salt

» crunchy roasted potatoes with rosemary

Preheat the oven to 220°C (425°F/Gas 7) and place the oven shelf in the middle.

Cut the potatoes in half and place in a large bowl with the oil, rosemary and sea salt. Toss to combine.

Place the potatoes, flat side down, in a single layer in a roasting pan, cover with foil and bake for 20 minutes. Remove the foil and cook for another 15-20 minutes.

Using a metal spatula, turn the potatoes over. Roast for another 15 minutes or until the potatoes are very golden and crisp.

4 SERVINGS

4 young celery stalks, including leaves, thinly sliced on the angle
2 French shallots, thinly sliced
3 red delicious apples, cored and cut into thin wedges
5 g (⅛ oz/¼ cup) flat-leaf (Italian) parsley, torn
60 g (2¼ oz/½ cup) walnuts, lightly toasted and coarsely chopped
185 g (6½ oz/¾ cup) good-quality mayonnaise
2 tablespoons lemon juice

» classic waldorf salad

Combine the celery, shallots, apple, parsley and walnuts in a bowl. Combine the mayonnaise and lemon juice in another bowl, then stir through the apple salad and season to taste just before serving.

1 kg (2 lb 4 oz) large all-purpose potatoes, such
   as desiree
1 teaspoon sea salt
80 ml (2½ fl oz/⅓ cup) olive oil
50 g (1¾ oz) butter

pan fried rosti «

Peel and wash the potatoes. Cut in half, place in a saucepan, cover with cold water and bring to the boil. Cover with tight-fitting lid and remove from the heat. Set aside for 10 minutes for the potatoes to soften. Drain well and cool.

Coarsely grate the potatoes into a bowl. Add the sea salt and stir to combine.

Heat half the oil and half the butter in a large non-stick frying pan over high heat. When the butter melts and sizzles, swirl the pan around to coat the sides. Add the grated potato and gently press down into the pan. Cook for 5 minutes.

Give the pan a couple of firm shakes, then reduce the heat to medium and cook for 10 minutes.

Use a plate slightly larger than the pan to sit on top of the pan. Carefully tip the pan over to invert the rosti on the plate.

Add the remaining oil and butter to the pan and place over medium heat. When the butter melts and sizzles, swirl the pan to coat the sides. Carefully slide the rosti back into the pan, so the golden cooked side is facing up and cook for another 10 minutes, shaking the pan occasionally.

4 SERVINGS

65 g (2½ oz) butter, softened
1 teaspoon coarsely snipped chives
1 tablespoon roughly chopped flat-leaf
   (Italian) parsley

4 cobs of corn
2 tablespoons olive oil

corn on the cob with herb butter «

Combine the butter and herbs in a small bowl and set aside. Bring a large saucepan of water to the boil, add the corn and cook for 5 minutes, then drain well and serve with the herb butter and season with sea salt and black pepper.

Heat the olive oil in a heavy-based frying pan over medium heat. Add the corn and cook, turning often, for 2 minutes. Remove from the pan, place on a serving plate, brush all over with the herb butter and season with sea salt and black pepper.

4 SERVINGS

75 g (2½ oz/½ cup) crumbled blue cheese
60 ml (2 fl oz/¼ cup) buttermilk
60 g (2¼ fl oz/¼ cup) light sour cream
2 tablespoons good-quality mayonnaise
1 teaspoon white wine vinegar
½ iceberg lettuce

» lettuce wedges with blue cheese dressing

Place the cheese and buttermilk in a small bowl and mash with a fork until well combined but still a little lumpy. Stir in the sour cream, mayonnaise and vinegar.

To serve, cut the lettuce into four thick wedges and spoon the dressing over the top.

4 SERVINGS

2 white onions, thinly sliced
½ teaspoon dried oregano
1 teaspoon caster (superfine) sugar
2 tablespoons white wine vinegar
1 teaspoon sea salt
4 thick slices sourdough bread
6 ripe tomatoes
60 ml (2 fl oz/¼ cup) extra virgin olive oil

» tomato, onion & bread salad

Place the onion, oregano, sugar, vinegar and sea salt in a bowl and toss to combine, separating the onion rings. Cover and refrigerate for at least 3 hours.

Toast the bread until golden and allow to cool. Roughly tear into small pieces.

Slice the tomatoes and place in a bowl with the torn bread, onion mixture and olive oil. Toss to combine, the season to taste with freshly ground black pepper and serve.

2 tablespoons red wine vinegar
2 teaspoons dijon mustard
330 g (11½ oz/8 cups) baby English spinach leaves
60 ml (2 fl oz/¼ cup) light olive oil

6 rashers bacon, rind removed, cut into 5 mm
  (¼ in)-wide strips
1 red onion, thinly sliced
1 clove garlic, crushed

warm spinach & bacon salad «

Combine the vinegar and mustard in a small bowl. Place the spinach leaves in a large serving bowl.

Heat the oil in a frying pan over high heat and cook the bacon for 5-6 minutes or until crisp. Add the onion and cook for 2 minutes or until soft. Remove from the heat and stir through the garlic.

While still warm, pour the bacon mixture onto the spinach leaves, including all the oil. Add the mustard mixture and toss to combine-the spinach leaves should just start to wilt and soften. Season to taste with black pepper and serve immediately.

4 SERVINGS

1 small head cauliflower, cut into florets
60 g (2¼ oz) butter
35 g (1¼ oz/¼ cup) plain (all-purpose) flour
500 ml (17 fl oz/2 cups) milk
125 g (4½ oz/1 cup) grated cheddar cheese

cauliflower mornay «

Bring a saucepan of lightly salted water to the boil. Add the cauliflower florets and cook for 4-5 minutes or until just tender. Drain well.

Preheat the oven to 180°C (350°F/Gas 4).

Heat the butter in a small saucepan over medium heat until sizzling and melted. Add the flour and stir for 1 minute. Remove the pan from the heat and slowly stir in the milk. Return the pan to the heat and stir for 2-3 minutes or until thick

and smooth. Add half the cheese and stir until melted and smooth.

Spoon half the sauce into the base of a shallow 1.5 litre (52 fl oz/6 cup) capacity oven proof dish. Put the cauliflower on top, then spoon over the remaining sauce. Sprinkle the remaining cheddar evenly over the top and then bake for 20-25 minutes or until golden.

4 SERVINGS

2 cloves garlic, crushed
20 g (¾ oz) butter, softened to room temperature
1.5 kg (3 lb 5 oz) all-purpose potatoes, such as desiree
500 ml (17 fl oz/2 cups) pouring (whipping) cream

» potato gratin

Preheat the oven to 180°C (350°F/Gas 4). Rub half the crushed garlic all over the base and sides of a 2.5 litre (87 fl oz/10 cup) capacity ceramic baking dish. Let it dry for a few minutes, then rub the butter all over the dish.

Peel the potatoes and slice as thinly as you can, about 2–3 mm (¹⁄₁₆–⅛ in) thick.

Place the cream and remaining garlic in a large saucepan and bring to the boil over medium heat. Reduce the heat to low and simmer for 10 minutes. Add the potatoes and stir gently to coat the potatoes in the cream without breaking them up. Increase the heat to high, return to the boil and remove from the heat. Season to taste.

Spoon the mixture into the baking dish, so the potato slices lay flat in the dish. Cover with foil and bake for 15 minutes. Remove the foil and cook for another 20–25 minutes or until the top is starting to turn golden around the edges.

4 SERVINGS

1 large sweet potato, peeled
125 ml (4 fl oz/½ cup) pouring (whipping) cream
80 g (2¾ oz) unsalted butter
½ teaspoon sea salt
¼ teaspoon freshly ground black pepper
2 tablespoons maple syrup
2 tablespoons dark rum

» rum & maple mashed sweet potato

Cut the sweet potato into 3–4 cm (1¼ in–1½ in) pieces and place in a saucepan with the cream, butter, sea salt and freshly ground black pepper. Partially cover the pan and cook over low heat for 30–35 minutes or until the sweet potatoes are very soft and falling apart. Remove from the heat and mash until smooth. Stir through the maple syrup and rum.

1 kg (2 lb 4 oz) button mushrooms
2 tablespoons olive oil
75 g (2½ oz) butter
1 clove garlic, crushed
1 tablespoon roughly chopped tarragon
¼ cup finely chopped flat-leaf (Italian) parsley
½ teaspoon sea salt

mushrooms with tarragon «

Trim any of the larger stems from the mushrooms and discard.

Heat the oil and butter in a large frying pan over high heat. When the butter has melted and starts to sizzle, add the mushrooms and garlic and cook for 5 minutes, shaking the pan often. Add the herbs and sea salt and cook for another 2 minutes or until tender.

4 SERVINGS

4 large leeks
500 ml (17 fl oz/2 cups) pouring (whipping) cream
1 clove garlic, crushed
2 tablespoons finely sliced mint

creamed leeks «

Preheat the oven to 220°C (425°F/Gas 7) and lightly butter a small 1 litre (35 fl oz/4 cup) capacity ovenproof dish.

Trim the leeks, discarding the green tops and slice the white parts into 4-5 cm (1½-2 in) long batons about 1 cm (½ in) wide. Bring a saucepan of lightly salted water to the boil and cook the leek for 3-4 minutes, until soft and silky. Drain very well and set aside.

Place the cream and garlic in a saucepan and bring to the boil over medium heat. Reduce the heat to low and cook for 15 minutes or until reduced to about 170 ml (5½ fl oz/⅔ cup) of a cup. Add the leeks and mint, season to taste and stir until well combined. Spoon into the baking dish and bake for 15-20 minutes or until golden and bubbling.

4 SERVINGS

6 desiree potatoes, peeled
2 litres (70 fl oz) canola oil
¼ teaspoon paprika
¼ teaspoon ground cumin
¼ teaspoon garlic salt

» spiced fries

Cut the round ends and sides off the potatoes to be roughly square. Cut the potatoes lengthways into 1.5 cm (⅝ in) wide pieces. Stack these on top of each other and cut lengthways again into 1.5 cm (⅝ in) wide chips. Place the chips in a sieve or colander and rinse under cold water to remove excess starch. Drain well and spread the chips over a clean teatowel. Put another towel on top and gently press down to dry very well.

Place the chips and oil in a large heavy-based saucepan over high heat. Stir with kitchen tongs to separate. Cook until the oil starts to boil, then cook for 10-15 minutes or until the potatoes look slightly limp.

Use tongs to gently stir and separate the chips, removing any that are stuck to the bottom of the pan. Cook for another 5-10 minutes or until the chips are golden and crisp. Use a slotted spoon to remove the chips and drain on paper towel.

Place the fries in a large metal bowl. Add the paprika, cumin and garlic salt and toss to coat. Serve immediately.

4 SERVINGS

200 g (7 oz) green beans, trimmed
2 zucchini (courgettes), thickly sliced on the angle
2 tablespoons olive oil
75 g (2½ oz) unsalted butter, chopped
15 g (½ oz/¼ cup) thinly sliced mint leaves

» buttered zucchini & beans with mint

Bring a saucepan of lightly salted water to the boil. Add the beans and cook for 1 minute, then add the zucchini and cook for 2 minutes. Drain well. Heat the olive oil in a large frying pan over high heat. Add the zucchini and cook for 2-3 minutes, turning once, or until golden on both sides. Remove from the heat, add the beans, butter and mint and season to taste.

80 ml (2½ fl oz/⅓ cup) olive oil
2 teaspoons dijon mustard
2 teaspoons red wine vinegar
½ teaspoon crushed garlic
360 g (4¼ oz/8 cups) good-quality salad mix

salad with red wine vinaigrette 《

Place the oil, mustard, vinegar, garlic and salt and freshly ground black pepper to taste in a small jar with a tight-fitting lid. Shake well to combine and refrigerate for up to 2 days. Remove from the refrigerator 30 minutes before using.

Place the salad leaves in a large bowl. Shake the dressing, pour over the salad and toss gently to combine.

4 SERVINGS

4 large beetroot (beets), about 170 g (6 oz) each
2 tablespoons prepared horseradish
1 tablespoon finely chopped tarragon, plus extra leaves, to serve
125 g (4½ fl oz/½ cup) light sour cream

baked beetroot with horseradish crème 《

Preheat the oven to 180°C (350°F/Gas 4).

Peel the beetroot. Firmly wrap each beetroot in two layers of foil, place on an oven tray and bake for 1 hour 15 minutes or until very tender and a skewer withdraws easily. Allow to cool in the foil for 15 minutes.

Combine the horseradish, tarragon and sour cream in a bowl. Season to taste.

Cut a deep cross in the top of each beetroot, gently prying open to make a cavity for the horseradish crème. Spoon the crème into each warm beetroot, scatter with extra tarragon leves and a grind of black pepper and serve immediately.

4 SERVINGS

150 g (5½ oz/1 cup) plain (all-purpose) flour
1 teaspoon baking powder
1 egg, lightly beaten
250 ml (9 fl oz/1 cup) cold beer
2 large brown onions
canola oil, for deep frying
sea salt flakes, for sprinkling

» onion rings

Combine the flour, baking powder and 1 teaspoon salt in a bowl, then make a well in the centre. Add the egg and beer and beat to make a smooth batter. Set aside for 30 minutes.

Slice the onions into 5 mm (¼ in)-thick rings, then place in a large bowl and toss to separate the rings.

Pour enough oil in a large saucepan or wok to come halfway up the sides and place over medium heat. The oil is ready when a drop of batter sizzles upon contact.

Working in batches, dip a handful of onion rings in the batter, allowing the excess to drain, then cook in the oil for 3–4 minutes or until golden and crisp. Drain on paper towel, sprinkle with sea salt flakes and serve immediately.

4 SERVINGS

125 g (4½ oz) butter
3 cloves garlic, crushed
750 g (1 lb 10 oz) floury potatoes, such
    as kennebec, peeled and quartered
60 ml (2 fl oz/¼ cup) warm milk
1 teaspoon sea salt

» garlicky mash

Place the butter and garlic in a small saucepan and cook over medium heat until the butter has just melted. Set aside for the garlic to soften and flavour the butter.

Meanwhile, bring a saucepan of lightly salted water to the boil. Add the potatoes and cook for 15–20 minutes or until tender and almost falling apart. Drain well, then return to the warm pan. Add the garlic butter, milk and sea salt. Mash until well combined but still a little chunky. Take a large wooden spoon and beat the mixture until it is smooth and creamy.

40 g (1½ oz) butter, melted
½ teaspoon thyme, plus extra sprigs, to serve
4 ripe truss tomatoes, halved
4 flat field mushrooms

baked mushrooms & tomatoes «

Preheat the oven to 220°C (425°F/Gas 7).

Combine the butter and thyme in a small bowl. Place the tomatoes, cut side up, on an oven tray. Add the mushrooms, capside down.

Brush with the butter and season well with salt and pepper. Bake for 20-25 minutes or until the tomatoes have softened. Scatter with extra thyme sprigs and serve.

4 SERVINGS

12 brussels sprouts, halved
1 tablespoon olive oil
60 g (2¼ oz) butter
2 rashers bacon, thinly sliced
2 cloves garlic, crushed

brussels sprouts with bacon «

Bring a saucepan of lightly salted water to the boil. Add the sprouts and cook for 5 minutes. Drain well.

Heat the oil and butter in a large frying pan over high heat. When the butter is sizzling, add the bacon and cook for 4-5 minutes or until crisp. Stir in the garlic and cook for 1 minute or until

aromatic. Add the sprouts and stir for 2-3 minutes or until heated through and evenly coated in the garlicky oil and bacon. Season to taste with sea salt and freshly ground black pepper.

sweets 191

There is never any holding back here and a bowl of cold fruit salad will just not do. Unless the fruit had first been macerated in some booze and topped with a sweetened cream, like the strawberries romanoff, the ultimate old-school sweet. Or you could gently soften some sliced summer peaches in port, ready to go in a trifle. But if it is winter fruit you like, you cannot go past a traditional apple strudel. For a bit of fun, set up a dessert trolley or sideboard with new york baked cheesecake, warm chocolate brownies and apple pie. A couple of jugs of cream and a bowl of vanilla ice cream on the side and all your sweet bases are covered. But there are some things which demand centre stage. These divas need no support act. The bombe alaska will be a show stopper and don't be surprised if you get a standing ovation … especially if it has sparklers!

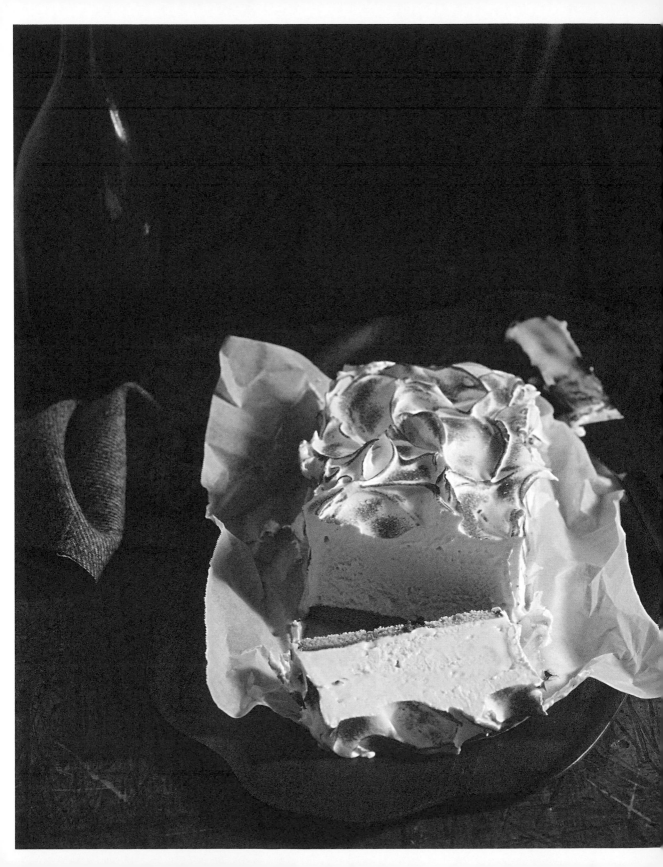

4 SERVINGS

1 litre (35 fl oz/4 cups) vanilla ice cream
1 madeira cake, about 450 g (1 lb) (or use
   sponge or sally cake)
200 g (7 oz) caster (superfine) sugar
5 egg whites
pinch cream of tartar

bombe alaska «

Remove the ice cream from the freezer and allow to soften slightly so it can be spooned out easily.

Line a 1.5 litre (52 fl oz/6 cup) capacity loaf (bar) tin with plastic wrap, with the sides overhanging so you can easily lift out the ice cream once it is frozen. Spoon the softened ice cream into the loaf tin, leaving about 2 cm (¾ in) at the top. Cut the madeira cake into 2 cm (¾ in)-thick slices, then place on top of the ice cream to cover, trimming to fit. Press down firmly, fold the plastic wrap over and freeze overnight.

The following day, place the sugar and 200 ml (7 fl oz) of water in a saucepan and stir over medium heat until the sugar dissolves. Brush the sides of the pan with a wet pastry brush to remove any grains of sugar. Simmer, without stirring but swirling the pan gently from time to time, until the mixture reaches 110-120°C (225-235°F) on a sugar thermometer or until it starts to turn a pale golden colour around the edges. Remove the mixture from the heat, give it one last swirl and leave it in the pan.

Using electric beaters, whisk the egg whites and cream of tartar until soft peaks form. With the motor running, pour the hot syrup into the meringue in a thin steady stream. Beat for 10-15 minutes or until thick and cool.

Working quickly, remove the frozen ice-cream log from the tin and invert onto a baking paper-lined oven tray. Using a spatula, spread the meringue over the ice cream, then use the back of a spoon to create peaks. Use a kitchen blowtorch to cook the meringue to an even golden colour all over. Cut into thick slices and serve immediately.

8–10 SERVINGS

125 g (4½ oz) plain, sweet biscuits, crushed
1 tablespoon sugar
60 g (2¾ oz) unsalted butter, melted
900 g (2 lb) cream cheese, softened to room temperature
80 g (2¾ oz/⅓ cup) thick (double/heavy) cream
350 g (12 oz) caster (superfine) sugar
1 teaspoon natural vanilla extract
2 teaspoons lemon juice
2 egg yolks
6 eggs

» new york baked cheesecake

Preheat the oven to 180°C (350°F/Gas 4). Lightly grease the base and sides of a 22 cm (8½ in) springform cake tin and line the base with baking paper.

Place the biscuit crumbs, white sugar and melted butter in a food processor and process until well combined. Tip into the cake tin. Use the base of a glass to press the mixture firmly into the base and 1.5 cm (⅝ in) up the sides of the tin. Bake for 10-12 minutes or until the mixture has the aroma of freshly baked biscuits. Remove from the oven and stand until cool.

Increase the oven temperature to 240°C (475°F/Gas 8).

Using an electric mixer, beat the cream cheese for 4-5 minutes or until almost lump-free, scraping the sides of the bowl down from time to time. Add the cream and beat for 1 minute, then add the caster sugar in two batches, beating for about 1 minute after each addition. Add the vanilla and lemon juice and beat to combine. Add the egg yolks and beat for 2-3 minutes. Add the eggs, one at a time, beating for a few seconds after each.

Pour the mixture into the cake tin and bake for 10 minutes. Reduce the oven temperature to 120°C (235°F/Gas ½) and bake for another 1½ hours or until the cake is puffed and golden. Remove to a wire rack to cool for 10-15 minutes. Carefully run a knife between the cake and the tin. Allow to cool to room temperature. Loosely wrap the cheesecake in foil and refrigerate until chilled. Remove the cake from the refrigerator 30 minutes before slicing.

3 eggs
½ teaspoon vanilla extract
1 tablespoon cornflour (cornstarch)
115 g (4 oz/½ cup) caster (superfine) sugar,
    plus 2 tablespoons extra
500 ml (17 fl oz/2 cups) milk

4 peaches, halved, seeded and thinly sliced
125 ml (4 fl oz/½ cup) port or sweet sherry
300 g (10½ oz) jam swiss rolls, cut into ½ cm
    (⅝ in)-thick slices
250 ml (9 fl oz/1 cup) pouring (whipping) cream
50 g (1¾ oz) flaked almonds, lightly toasted

port wine trifle «

Combine the eggs, vanilla, cornflour and 110 g (3¾ oz/½ cup) of the sugar in a heatproof bowl set over a saucepan of just simmering water, making sure the water does not come into contact with the bottom of the bowl. Whisk for 5 minutes or until thick and pale. Add the milk and continue to beat until the custard is thick. Remove, cover closely with plastic wrap and allow to cool.

Place the peaches, sherry and extra sugar in a frying pan and cook over medium heat for 5 minutes or until the sugar has dissolved and the peaches are slightly softened. Remove from the heat and cool. Drain the peaches and reserve the syrup. Arrange half the peach slices in the base of a deep glass serving dish and pour over the remaining syrup.

Arrange the cake slices around the side of the dish and the remaining cake slices on top of the peaches. Pour over half the reserved syrup, spoon custard over the top and arrange the remaining peaches on top of the custard.

Whisk the cream until firm peaks form, spoon over the custard. Chill for several hours before serving with the almonds scattered on top.

50 g (1¾ oz) raisins
60 ml (2 fl oz/¼ cup) brandy
4 tart green apples, 500 g (1 lb 2 oz), such as granny smiths,
    peeled, cored and thinly sliced
1 teaspoon finely grated lemon zest
2 tablespoons lemon juice
40 g (1½ oz/½ cup) fresh breadcrumbs
95 g (3¼ oz/½ cup) soft brown sugar
1 teaspoon ground cinnamon
10 sheets filo pastry (28 x 45 cm/11¼ × 18 in)
150 g (5½ oz) unsalted butter, melted
60 g (2¼ oz/½ cup) icing (confectioners') sugar
thick cream, to serve

» apple strudel with cream

Place the raisins and brandy in a small bowl and soak for 1 hour. Drain well, discard the liquid and combine the raisins in a bowl with the apple, lemon zest and juice. Set aside.

Combine the breadcrumbs, brown sugar and cinnamon in a bowl.

Lay a sheet of filo on a work surface and keep the others covered to prevent drying out. Brush all over with 1 tablespoon of melted butter. Top with another sheet of filo, then repeat with the butter and filo until all the sheets of filo are buttered and stacked on top of each other. Lightly brush the top sheet of filo with butter.

Preheat the oven to 180°C (350°F/Gas 4).

Sprinkle the breadcrumb mixture evenly over the filo, leaving 5 cm (2 in) border from the edge.

With one long end towards you, spoon the apple mixture onto bottom end into a neat and even log. Roll the filo up and over the apple mixture, folding in the sides as you go, making sure they are firmly tucked in. Place the strudel, seam side down, on a baking paper-lined oven tray. Brush all over with the remaining melted butter and finely and evenly sift the icing sugar all over the log. Bake for 45 minutes or until the pastry is golden and firm when gently tapped. Serve warm or at room temperature with cream.

250 ml (9 fl oz/1 cup) bourbon
125 g (4½ oz/1 cup) raisins
1 teaspoon bicarbonate of soda
80 g (2¾ oz) unsalted butter, softened
165 g (5¾ oz) raw caster (superfine) sugar
2 eggs, lightly beaten
185 g (6½ oz/1¼ cups) plain (all-purpose)
  flour, sifted

1 teaspoon baking powder
thick (double/heavy) cream, to serve

BUTTERSCOTCH SAUCE
150 g (5½ oz) soft brown sugar
170 ml (5½ fl oz/⅔ cup) pouring
  (whipping) cream
30 g (1 oz) unsalted butter

bourbon & raisin pudding «
with butterscotch sauce

Place the bourbon and 60 ml (2 fl oz/¼ cup) water in a small saucepan and bring to the boil. Put the raisins and bicarbonate of soda in a heatproof bowl. Pour over the hot bourbon, cover and set aside for 30 minutes.

Preheat the oven to 180°C (350°F/Gas 4). Grease four shallow 250 ml (9 fl oz/1 cup) capacity ovenproof dishes.

Using an electric mixer, beat the butter and sugar for 3-4 minutes or until light and fluffy. Add the eggs and beat for 1 minute, then add the flour and baking powder and combine well. Stir through the raisin mixture and spoon into the greased

dishes. Bake for 20 minutes or until a skewer withdraws clean. Stand for 10 minutes while making the sauce.

For the butterscotch sauce, place all the ingredients in a small saucepan and stir over medium heat until melted and smooth.

Pour the hot butterscotch sauce over the puddings and serve with thick cream on the side.

4 SERVINGS

500 g (1 lb 2 oz) strawberries, hulled and halved if large
60 ml (2 fl oz/¼ cup) freshly squeezed orange juice
60 ml (2 fl oz/¼ cup) cointreau
50 g (1¾ oz/¼ cup) caster (superfine) sugar
125 ml (4 fl oz/½ cup) whipping cream

» strawberries romanoff

Place the strawberries in a non-metallic bowl with the orange juice, cointreau and half the sugar. Cover and then refrigerate for up to 3 hours, stirring often.

Whisk the cream and remaining sugar until firm peaks form. Spoon the berries and sauce into glasses and spoon the cream over.

200 g (7 oz) dark chocolate (min 70% cocoa)
125 g (4½ oz) unsalted butter
30 g (1 oz/¼ cup) unsweetened cocoa powder,
    sifted, plus extra, for dusting
3 eggs
220 g (7¾ oz/1 cup) raw (demerara) sugar
1 teaspoon vanilla extract
125 g (4½ oz) plain (all-purpose) flour, sifted
thick (double/heavy) cream, or vanilla ice cream,
    to serve

warm chocolate brownie «

Preheat the oven to 180°C (350°F/Gas 4). Grease and line a 20 cm (8 in) square cake tin with baking paper, making sure some of the baking paper overhangs the sides.

Place the chocolate and butter in a heatproof bowl set over a saucepan of just simmering water, making sure the bottom of the bowl does not come into contact with the water. Stir occasionally until both the butter and chocolate are melted and smooth. Remove from the heat, add the cocoa and stir until smooth, then set aside.

Beat the eggs, sugar and vanilla until just combined. Stir into the chocolate mixture, then fold in the flour until well combined and smooth. Pour into the tin and bake for 30–35 minutes or until set around the edges. The brownie should still be wobbly in the centre. Allow to cool in the tin for 15–20 minutes. Use the baking paper to lift the brownie out of the tin. Dust with extra cocoa powder. Cut into squares and serve warm with thick cream or vanilla ice cream.

8 SERVINGS

800 g (1 lb 12 oz) granny smith apples
800 g (1 lb 12 oz) other green apples
   (golden delicious or mcintosh)
165 g (5¾ oz) caster (superfine) sugar,
   plus 2 teaspoons extra
2 tablespoons lemon juice
¼ teaspoon allspice
¼ teaspoon ground cinnamon

2 tablespoons cornflour (cornstarch)
150 g (5½ oz) aged cheddar cheese, thinly sliced
1 egg white, lightly beaten

PASTRY
300 g (10½ oz/2 cups) plain (all-purpose) flour
2 tablespoons sugar
200 g (7 oz) unsalted butter, chilled and cubed

» apple & cheddar pie

For the pastry, place the flour and sugar in a food processor and pulse to combine. With the motor running, add several cubes of butter at a time until all the butter has been added but do not over process. Add 2-3 tablespoons iced water or just enough to bring the dough together and pulse until the mixture just starts to come together. Tip onto a lightly floured surface and knead for 1 minute or until smooth. Divide into two equal portions and roll each into two discs, about 10 cm (4 in) across. Wrap in plastic wrap and refrigerate for at least 30 minutes or up to one day.

Remove the pastry from the refrigerator 30 minutes before rolling. Preheat the oven to 220°C (425°F/Gas 7) and lightly grease a 23-24 cm (9-9½ in) pie dish or 6 x 1 cup capacity baking dish.

Roll out one disc of dough between two sheets of baking paper into a 30 cm (12 in) circle. Remove the top piece of paper, then place the pastry round, with the bottom piece of paper underneath into the dish and gently press into the edges, allowing the sides to overhang. Transfer to the refrigerator while preparing the apple filling.

Peel, core and thinly slice both apple varieties. Place in a bowl with the sugar, lemon juice, spices and cornflour and use your hands to combine well. Tip the mixture into the pie dish, making a high mound in the centre. Arrange the cheddar slices all over the apples.

Roll out the other piece of dough between two sheets of baking paper until it is large enough to entirely cover the pie dish. Sit the pastry on top. Trim and crimp the edges with a fork. Brush the pastry with the egg white, sprinkle the extra sugar evenly on top then bake for 20 minutes. Reduce the oven temperature to 180°C (350°F/Gas 4) and bake for another 25 minutes or until the pastry is golden. Allow to cool in the dish for 30-45 minutes. Slice and serve warm.

There is an element of fun to this food. I for one am very happy that this delicious, tasty style of cooking has come full circle and that it's okay to eat salty chicken skin, crispy pork belly, custard and cream again. Of course, I don't mean okay in the sense that it is good for us – naturally we shouldn't eat like this every day … but every now and then, throw caution to the wind. Cook, eat up and enjoy.

» index

Published in 2010 by Murdoch Books Pty Limited

Murdoch Books Australia
Pier 8/9, 23 Hickson Road
Millers Point NSW 2000
Phone: +61 (0) 2 8220 2000
Fax: +61 (0) 2 8220 2558
www.murdochbooks.com.au

Murdoch Books UK Limited
Erico House, 6th Floor
93-99 Upper Richmond Road
Putney, London SW15 2TG
Phone: +44 (0) 20 8785 5995
Fax: +44 (0) 20 8785 5985
www.murdochbooks.co.uk

Publisher: Kay Scarlett
Concept and design: Reuben Crossman
Photographer: Brett Stevens
Stylist: David Morgan
Project editor: Livia Caiazzo
Food consultant: Christine Osmond
Production: Joan Beal

Murdoch Books wishes to thank Laminex
(contact 132 136 or www.laminex.com.au) for use of
their products for photography.

National Library of Australia Cataloguing-in-Publication
Data:

Author: Dobson, Ross, 1965-
Title: Grillhouse / Ross Dobson.
ISBN: 9781741967142 (hbk.)
Notes: Includes index.
Subjects: Barbecue cookery
Dewey Number: 641.5784

A catalogue record for this book is available from the
British Library.

Colour separation by Splitting Image
Reprinted 2010, 2011 (twice).

IMPORTANT: Those who might be at risk from the effects
of salmonella poisoning (the elderly, pregnant women,
young children and those suffering from immune
deficiency diseases) should consult their doctor with any
concerns about eating raw eggs.

OVEN GUIDE: You may find cooking times vary depending
on the oven you are using. For fan-forced ovens, as a general
rule, set the oven temperature to 20°C (35°F) lower than
indicated in the recipe.